Aberdeenshire Library and Information Service
www.aberdeenshire.gov.uk/alis
Renewals Hotline 01224 661511

24 JUL 2009 ~ SEP 2009

15/12/08
17 JAN 2009

1 0 FEB 2009   31 OCT 2009

1 4 MAR 2009   1 9 DEC 2009

27 JAN 2010

- 2 DEC 2010

- 6 APR 2009   2 5 FEB 2010

2 7 APR 2010

1 3 MAY 2009   1 7 MAY 2010

- 7 AUG 2009

1 7 JUN 2010

2 1 AUG 2010

DAY, Chrissie

Quick crochet

Quick Crochet

35 fast, fun projects to make in a weekend

Chrissie Day

CICO BOOKS

LONDON NEW YORK

Published in 2007 by CICO Books
an imprint of Ryland Peters & Small
20–21 Jockey's Fields, London WC1R 4BW

www.cicobooks.co.uk

10 9 8 7 6 5 4 3 2 1

A CIP catalogue record for this book is available from
the British Library

ISBN-13: 978 1 904991 92 2
ISBN-10: 1 904991 92 0

Printed in China

Editor: Marie Clayton
Designer: Roger Hammond
Photographers: Paul Bricknall, Geoff Dann and Tino Tedaldi

contents

introduction

In an age of high technology it is refreshing to know that one of the oldest crafts – crochet – has not only survived but has a fresh new following wanting to learn and explore. I have crocheted for about as long as I have knitted and, in this world where speed is essential, it seems comforting to know that crochet work is quicker than knitting. Once the basics have been mastered, 'the sky's the limit' as new textures, new patterns beckon you to try, as well as all the possible materials: cottons, linens, raffia, leather, wire, silks. Whether you are making a piece in fine cotton or silk or using chunky wool, the stitch is the same and it is the same language in any country – crochet is universal.

As always, each piece starts as a sketch – an idea in my sketch book – and it is only when I have finished this process that it is taken further as yarn is introduced and the decision taken that a crochet stitch is needed for the item. In this book you will find differing projects, which I hope will excite you and hasten you to get out your hook and give it a try. Choice of colours and yarns is always hard and I hope the colours I have chosen in this book inspire you – but do not be afraid to do these designs in

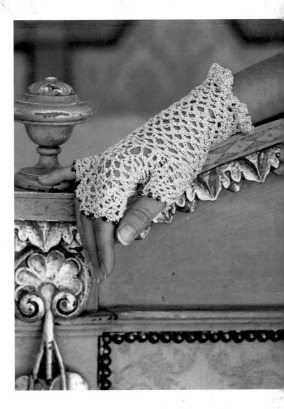

other colourways. Colour is personal, so never be afraid to change what you see on the page to a colour that suits you or that you like better.

I love experimenting by adding other fibres and pushing the medium by combining other materials and techniques in unusual ways. Think outside the box and invent your own ways to use these patterns with differing textures. Crochet is addictive, yet calming, and will help you be at one with the ups and downs of life – let it into your life and enjoy the journey!

I think if my stitches were tears I would have crocheted an ocean by now, but equally much of my work is interlaced with love and soft memories – the golden times of the present and the past worked into every stitch, binding the garment together. I dedicate this book to all those who have ever taught me and shown me the way.

hats, wraps and gloves

The right hat, wrap or pair of gloves in a pleasing yarn that suits the wearer does so much more than just enhance an outfit. The projects in this chapter include a range of very different hats, some wonderfully textured scarves and wraps, a luxurious shrug, sparkly arm warmers and a pretty pair of lacy gloves.

A hat denotes your mood of the moment – which can change as much as you want it to! Feel glamorous in the soft Cashmere Helmet that fits closely to your head, or bring back memories of the Bloomsbury set with the Silky Cloche Hat. Crochet lends itself to creating wonderful textures and these have been my starting point for many of the projects in this book. The Curlique-end Scarf has cascades of twists at each end, while the Bobble Hat is a riot of texture all over.

The wonderful yarns now on offer also offer constant inspiration – colours, textures, silk, alpaca, cashmere, merino – the variety available is almost endless. So express your creativity and enjoy the exciting projects on the following pages.

Materials

1 x 100g ball of Wensleydale DK, colour 123 cerise (A)
1 x 100g ball of Wensleydale DK, colour 154 aubergine (B)
3.50mm (E/4) crochet hook
Piece of cardboard to make the tassel
Yarn needle

Size

Approx 115cm (45in) after felting.

Tension

Tension is not important on this project, as the finished piece will be felted.

Abbreviations

ch chain
cont continue
dc double crochet
rep repeat
ss slip stitch
st(s) stitch(es)

Special instructions

To felt the scarf, wash in very hot water with liquid soap, rubbing gently with your hands until the fibres begin to matt together. Alternatively you can put it in the washing machine, but it is less easy to control the process. The rings will become smaller and firmer when felted, but be careful they do not stick together. For more detailed felting instructions, see page 76.

chain link felted scarf with tassels

The dramatic colours and bold shapes of this unusual scarf will bring you attention wherever you go! I love the rounded shapes in chunky chains and I have used them here to create a light, open scarf that is fun to wear.

CIRCLE 1

Using A, make 35ch, ss into first ch to form a ring.
Round 1: 1ch, 1dc into same place as ss, 1dc into each ch, ss into first dc, turn.
Round 2: 1ch, 1dc into each dc, ss into first dc, turn.
Rep this last round twice more.
Fasten off.

CIRCLE 2

As circle 1, but thread commencing ch through circle 1 before joining into ring.

CIRCLES 3–6

Make and join 1 more A circle and 3 B circles, joining circle 6 to circle 1.

CIRCLES 7–8

Join 1 A circle to first B circle and 1 A circle to 3rd B circle.

CIRCLES 9–10

Join 1 A circle to circle 7 and 1 A circle to circle 8, linking each through centre B circle.

CIRCLE 11

Join 1 A circle through both circles 9 and 10.

CIRCLE 12

Join 1 B circle through circles 9 and 11.

CIRCLE 13

Join 1 B circle through circles 10 and 11.

CIRCLE 14

Join 1 B circle through circles 11 and 12.

CIRCLE 15

Join 1 B circle through circles 11 and 13.

CIRCLE 16

Join 1 B circle through circles 14 and 15.

CIRCLE 17

Join 1 A circle through circle 14.

CIRCLE 18

Join 1 A circle through circle 15.
Cont in this way, changing colour after every 5 circles, until work measures approx 110cm (44in) ending with 1 circle linking 2 circles.

TASSEL

Using A and B, make a tassel 22cm (8¾in) long. Stitch the tassel to one end of the scarf and loop the last chain of the other end over it.

cerise rose shawl

A large stole trimmed with roses – a really pretty design for those warm summer evenings when you need romance in the air around you. The stole is made in three sections and the roses are used to join them for an open and light effect.

Materials

9 x 25g balls of Rowan Kidsilk Haze, candy girl (A)
1 x 25g ball of Rowan Kidsilk Haze, jelly (B)
3.50mm (E/4) crochet hook
Yarn needle

Size

92 x 148cm (36 x 58in)

Tension

16 sts and 9 rows to 10cm (4in) over dc using 3.50mm (E/4) hook.

Abbreviations

ch chain
ch sp chain space
dc double crochet
rem remaining
rep repeat
st(s) stitch(es)
tr treble crochet

STOLE

(Make 3 identical sections)
Using A make 52ch.
Row 1: 1tr in 4th ch, 1tr in each ch to end. (50 sts)
Row 2: Ch3 (counts as tr), 1tr in each tr.
Rep Row 2 until 133 rows or 148cm (58in) have been worked. Fasten off.

ROSES

(Make a selection in 3 sizes and varying colours including some using 1 strand of each colour together)
Using A, make 16 or 26 or 36ch.
Row 1: 1tr in 4th ch, *1ch, skip 1ch, (1tr, 1ch, 1tr) in next ch (V-stitch worked); rep until there are 6(11,16) V-sts.

Row 2: Ch3 (counts as tr), 5tr in first ch sp *1dc in next ch sp, 6tr in next ch sp, (shell stitch made); rep from * to end, 6tr in last ch sp.
Fasten off, leaving a long tail. Thread onto a needle and take down to first row, roll up first 1cm (⅜in) to form a bud, roll remainder and stitch down.

MAKING UP

Fasten the three sections together with crocheted roses. Line all three pieces up side-by-side. Slightly overlapping the upper layer on each, pin the two centres and attach rose at each. Attach remaining roses at intervals, to join sections. Fold top section over centre section and join top corners to lower corners of each centre section to make holes for arms.

Materials

3 × 50g balls of Twilleys Freedom, colour 408
5.00mm (H/8) crochet hook
6.00mm (J/10) crochet hook

Size

One size, to fit average adult head

Tension

11 sts and 13 rounds to 10cm (4in) over dc using 6.00mm (J/10) crochet hook.

Abbreviations

bl back loop
ch chain
dc double crochet
RS right side
ss slip stitch
st(s) stitch(es)
tr treble crochet
WS wrong side

Special abbreviations

MB – make bobble, always inserting the hook into the same st and leaving the last loop of each st on the hook, yarn around hook and draw through all the loops on the hook.

bobbles hat

Just wild bobbles everywhere on this funky and multicoloured hat! You will create a stir wherever you go while wearing it. The yarn is dyed to create the multicolour effect, so no need to worry about colour changes. The crown is topped with a cluster of loops for an unusual finishing touch.

HAT

Using 6.00mm (J/10) hook, make 3ch, into 3rd ch from hook work 6dc, ss into first dc of round, turn.

Round 1 (WS): 1ch, 2dc into each dc, ss into first dc, turn. (12 dc)

Round 2 (RS): 1ch, 2dc into each dc, ss into first dc of round, turn. (24 dc)

Round 3: 1ch, 1dc into each dc to end, ss into first dc, turn.

Round 4: 1ch, 1dc into each of first 2dc, [MB into next dc, 1dc into each of next 3dc] 5 times, MB into next dc, 1dc into last dc, ss into first dc, turn.

Round 5: 1ch, 1dc into first dc, [2dc into next dc, 1dc into next dc] to last dc, 2dc into last dc, ss into first dc, turn. (36 dc)

Round 6: 1ch, 1dc into each dc, ss into first dc, turn.

Round 7: 1ch, 1dc into each of first 2dc, 2dc into next dc, [1dc into each of next 2dc, 2dc into next dc] to end, ss into first dc, turn. (48 dc)

Round 8: As Round 6.

Round 9: 1ch, 1dc into each of first 3dc, 2dc into next dc, [1dc into each of next 3dc, 2dc into next dc] to end, ss into first dc, turn. (60 dc)

Round 10: As Round 5.

Round 11: 1ch, [1dc into each of next 9dc, 2dc into next dc] to end, ss into first dc, turn. (66 dc)

Round 12: 1ch, 1dc into each of first 5dc, [MB into next dc, 1dc into each of next 7dc] 7 times, MB into next dc, 1dc into each of last 4 dc, ss into first dc, turn.

Rounds 13–15: 1ch, 1dc into each dc, ss into first dc, turn.

Round 16: 1ch, 1dc into first dc, [MB into next dc, 1dc into each of next 7dc] 7 times, MB into next dc, 1dc into each of last 8 dc, ss into first dc, turn.

Rounds 17–19: As Rounds 13–15.

Rounds 20–23: As Rounds 12–15.

Do not fasten off.

Ribbing edge

Change to 5.00mm (H/8) hook.

Row 1: 5ch, 1dc into 2nd ch from hook, 1dc into each of 3ch, ss into next st of last round of hat body. (4 dc)

Row 2: Working into the bl only, 1dc into each of next 4 dc, turn.

Row 3: Still working into bl only, 1ch, 1dc into each of 4 dc, ss into each of next 2 sts of last row of hat, turn.

Rep Rows 2 and 3 until ribbing meets up to first row of rib.

On last row of ribbing, work through the bl and the opposite side of the foundation ch of the ribbing, ss into each of the 4 dc.

Fasten off.

MAKING UP

With RS of hat facing and 5.00mm (H/8) hook, join yarn to any dc of base row of hat, working around the top centre circle, [12ch, ss into next dc of circle] 5 times, 12ch, ss into first ss.

This forms a group of 6 loops into top circle of hat.

Fasten off.

Materials
4 x 50g balls of Colinette Cadenza, marble
5.00mm (H/8) crochet hook

Size
Length 78cm (30¾in); width 15cm (6in)

Tension
19 dc and 20 rows to 10cm (4in) over dc
using 5.00mm (H/8) hook.

Abbreviations
ch chain
dc double crochet
rep repeat
RS right side
ss slip stitch
st(s) stitch(es)
tr treble
WS wrong side
yrh yarn round hook

Special abbreviations
MB – make bobble, leaving last loop of
each tr on hook, work 7tr in same st, yrh
and draw through all the loops on the
hook. Push bobble through to RS.

curlicue-end scarf

I love texture, and here I have combined bobble with the twisted shapes of curlicues. Although it looks quite complex, this scarf is not that difficult to make – just remember to push the bobbles to the right side as they are made.

MAIN SECTION
Make 29ch.

Base row (RS): 1dc into 2nd ch from hook, 1dc into each ch to end. (28 dc)

Row 1: 1ch, 1dc into each dc to end, turn.

Rep last row until scarf measures 43cm (17in), ending with a WS row. Do not fasten off.

With RS of main section of scarf facing, make 31ch.

Curlicue ends

Base row: 1tr into 4th ch from hook, 1tr into each ch to end, turn. (29 sts)

Row 1 (WS): 1ch, 1dc into first 2tr, *MB into next tr, 1dc into each of next 3tr; rep from * to last 3sts, MB into next tr, 1dc into next tr, 1dc into top of 3ch, turn.

Row 2: 3ch (count as 1tr), miss first dc, 1tr into each st to end.

Row 3: 1ch, 1dc into first 4tr, *MB, 1dc into each of next 3tr; rep from * to last st, 1dc into top of 3ch, turn.

Row 4: As Row 2.

Rep Rows 1–4, ss in other corner of main section.

Fasten off.

Making tucks in end of main section, sew curlicue ends to main section. With RS facing, rejoin yarn to top of 3ch at beg of last row of curlicue end. 1ch, 1dc into first st, [14ch, 4tr into 4th ch from hook, 4tr into each ch, ss into last dc] (curlicue made), 1dc into next 2sts of curlicue end, work 1 curlicue as before, 1dc into next 3 sts; rep from * to start of main section omitting last rep, ending 1 curlicue in last st.

Fasten off.

Work along opposite edge of curlicue end to match. With RS facing, join yarn to right corner at other end of main section, make 31ch, then complete as other end.

MAKING UP
Press under a damp cloth on the main section only, leaving the curlicue ends unpressed.

Twisted curlicues and masses of bobbles create lots of texture

Materials
2 x 100g balls of Knitglobal Nazca Baby Alpaca, white (A)
2 x 100g balls of Knitglobal Nazca Baby Alpaca, black (B)
4.50mm (G/6) crochet hook

Size
152 x 37cm (60 x 14½in).

Tension
24 st to 15cm (6in) and 4 rows to 7cm (2¾in) over pattern, with 4.50mm (G/6) hook.

Abbreviations
ch chain
cont continue
patt pattern
rep repeat
ss slip stitch
st(s) stitch(es)
tch turning chain
tr treble

domino alpaca shawl

This classic black and white shawl will never date and was inspired by a set of dominos scattered across the carpet. I liked the strong contrast of the black dots on the white background, so I tried to achieve the same effect in this dramatic shawl. It is made in in the most wonderful super-soft baby Alpaca yarn.

SHAWL
Using A, make 246ch.
Row 1: With A, 1tr into 4th ch from hook, 1tr into each ch to end, turn. (244 sts)
Row 2: With B, 3ch, (count as 1tr), miss first tr, 1tr into each of next 5tr, 8ch, miss 8tr, *1tr into each of next 4tr, 8ch, miss 8tr; rep from * to last 2 sts, 1tr into last tr, 1tr into top of tch, turn.
Row 3: With B, 8ch, miss first 2tr and 4ch, 1tr into each of next 4ch, *8ch, miss next 4tr and 4ch, 1tr into each of next 4ch; rep from * to last 6 sts, 4ch, miss 4tr, 1tr into next tr, 1tr into top of tch, turn.
Row 4: With B, 3ch, (count as 1tr), miss first tr, 1tr into next tr, *1tr into each of next 4ch, 8ch, miss 4tr and 4ch; rep from * ending 1tr into eachof next 2ch, turn.
Cont in stripes of 4 rows A and 4 rows B.
Row 5: 3ch, (count as 1tr), miss first tr, 1tr into each tr and ch to end, 1tr into top of tch, turn. (244 sts)

Row 6: 3ch, (count as 1tr), miss first tr, 1tr into next tr, *8ch, miss 8tr, 1tr into each of next 4tr; rep from * to last 2 sts, 1ch, 1tr into next tr, 1tr into top of tch, turn.
Row 7: 3ch, (count as 1tr), miss first tr, 1tr into next tr, *8ch, miss next 4tr and 4ch, 1tr into each of next 4ch; rep from * to last 2 sts, 1tr into next tr, 1tr into top of tch, turn.
Row 8: 3ch, (count as 1tr), miss first tr, 1tr into next tr, *8ch, miss next 4tr and 4ch, 1tr into each of next 4ch; rep from * to last 2 sts, 1tr into next tr, 1tr into top of tch, turn.
Row 9: 3ch, (count as 1tr), miss first tr, 1tr into each tr and ch to end, turn. (244 tr)
Rep Rows 2–9 once, then Rows 2–5 once again.
Fasten off.

MAKING UP
Chain stitch around a few selected holes with opposite colour, as shown in photo. Leave ends after tying off.

*Classic black
and white will
never date*

sparkle arm warmers

The pretty ruffles at the cuffs of these seductive sparkly arm warmers add a touch of drama and femininity. Wear them with anything from evening dress to jeans – you'll never look out of place!

Materials
2 × 50g balls of Bouton d'or, colour 399 (A)
2 × 50g balls of Lantarus Queen, colour 071 (B)
4.00mm (F/5) crochet hook

Size
Upper arm width 29cm (11½in); length to wrist 38cm (15in), excluding frill.

Tension
5 patt repeats to 9 cm (3½in) × 26 rows to 10cm (4in) over pattern, using 4.00mm (F/5) hook.

Abbreviations
ch chain
ch sp chain space
dc double crochet
dec decrease
patt pattern
rep repeat
RS right side
ss slip stitch
st(s) stitch(es)
WS wrong side

GLOVES
(Make 2)
With A, make 64ch.
Row 1: 1dc into 4th ch from hook, *3ch, 1dc into next ch, 3ch, miss 2ch, 1dc into next ch; rep from * to end, turn. (15 patts)
Row 2: 3ch, *[1dc, 3ch, 1dc] into next 3ch sp, 3ch, miss next 3ch sp; rep from * ending with 1dc into last 3ch, turn.
Rep Row 2 twice more.
Taking dec into the pattern, work as follows:
Row 5 (dec row): Ss into first 3ch sp, 1ch, [1dc, 3ch, 1dc] into same 3ch sp, *3ch, miss next 3ch sp, [1dc, 3ch, 1dc] into next 3ch sp; rep from * ending with 3ch, 1dc into last 3ch, turn.
Row 6: Ss into first 3ch sp, 1ch, [1dc, 3ch, 1dc] into first 3ch sp, *3ch, miss next 3ch sp, [1dc, 3ch, 1dc] into next 3ch sp; rep from * to last 3ch sp, 3ch, 1dc into last dc, turn.
Rows 7–10: 1ch, [1dc, 3ch, 1dc] into first 3ch sp, *3ch, miss next 3ch sp, [1dc, 3ch, 1dc] into next 3ch sp; rep from * to last 3ch sp, 3ch, 1dc into last dc, turn.

Row 11 (dec row): 1ch, 1dc into first 3ch sp, *3ch, miss next 3ch sp, [1dc, 3ch, 1dc] into next 3ch sp; rep from * to last 3ch sp, 2ch, 1dc into last dc, turn.
Rows 12–16: 1ch, 1dc into first 2ch sp, *3ch, miss next 3ch sp, [1dc, 3ch, 1dc] into next 3ch sp; rep from * ending 1dc into last dc, turn.
Row 17 (dec row): Ss into 2nd dc, 1ch, 1dc into this dc, 2ch, miss next 3ch sp, *[1dc, 3ch, 1dc] into next 3ch sp, 3ch, miss next 3ch sp]; rep from * to last 3ch sp, [1dc, 3ch, 1dc] into this sp, 1ch, 1dc into last dc, turn.
Rows 18–22: 1ch, 1dc into first dc, 2ch, miss next 3ch sp, *[1dc, 3ch, 1dc] into next 3ch sp, 3ch, miss next 3ch sp; rep from * ending with [1dc, 3ch, 1dc] intonext 3ch sp, 2ch, miss last 3ch sp, 1dc into last dc, turn.
Row 23 (dec row): 3ch, miss first 3ch sp, *[1dc, 3ch, 1dc] into next 3ch sp, 3ch, miss 3ch sp; rep from * to last 2ch sp, working 1dc into last dc, turn.
Rows 24–28: 3ch, *[1dc, 3ch, 1dc] into next 3ch sp, 3ch, miss next 3ch sp; rep from * ending 1dc into last 3ch sp, turn.

Rep Rows 5 to 28 inclusive once more, then work straight as Row 2, until work measures 38cm (15in).

Cuff

Fasten off A, join in B.

Row 1: 3ch, *[1dc, 3ch, 1dc] into next 3ch sp, 3ch, 1dc into next 3ch sp, 3ch; rep from * to last 3ch sp, [1dc, 3ch, 1dc] into this sp, turn.

Row 2: 3ch, 1dc into first 3ch sp, *[3ch, (1dc, 3ch, 1dc) into next 3ch sp] twice, 3ch, 1dc into 3ch sp; rep from * to last 3ch sp, 3ch, [1dc, 3ch, 1dc] into this sp, turn.

Row 3: 3ch, 1dc into first 3ch sp, *[3ch, (1dc, 3ch, 1dc)] into next 3ch sp; rep from * to end, turn.

Row 4: 3ch, *[1dc, 3ch, 1dc] into 3ch sp, 3ch, miss next 3ch sp; rep from * ending 1dc into last 3ch sp, turn.

Rep Rows 3 and 4 once more.

Row 7: 3ch, [1dc, 3ch, 1dc] into first 3ch sp, *3ch, miss next 3ch sp, [1dc, 3ch, 1dc] into next 3ch sp; rep from * to end.

Row 8: 3ch, miss first 3ch sp, *[1dc, 3ch, 1dc] into next 3ch sp, 3ch, miss next 3ch sp; rep from * ending 1dc into last 3ch sp.

Fasten off.

MAKING UP

With WS facing, join seam.

summer days hat

Ice cream, candyfloss, seaside ponies, clapboard pastel-painted beach huts... and a floppy hat that will keep you cool under the hot sun, shade your eyes, make you feel good. This is certainly the one, crocheted in beautiful soft linen drape. Make several in a variety of pastel colours to go with all your summer outfits.

Materials
1 x 50g ball of Rowan Linen Drape, colour 861 (A)
1 x 50g ball of Rowan Linen Drape, colour 844 (B)
1 x 50g ball of Rowan Linen Drape, colour 845 (C)
2.75mm (C/2) crochet hook
3.50mm (E/4) crochet hook

Size
One size, to fit average adult head.

Tension
11dc x 12 rows to 5cm (2in) over dc using 2.75mm (C/2) hook.

Abbreviations
ch chain
dc double crochet
rep repeat
ss slip stitch
st(s) stitch(es)
yrh yarn round hook

Special abbreviations
Reverse dc (crab stitch) = dc worked from left to right. Insert hook into the next st to the right, yrh, pull the yarn through, twisting hook to face upwards at the same time, yrh and draw through to finish off the dc as normal. Working in this direction causes a twist that gives a decorative edge.

Notes

Work the following colour sequence throughout: A x 4 rounds; B x 2 rounds; C x 4 rounds.
Break off yarn after each band of colour and weave into stitches.
The hat is worked as one piece.

HAT

Using 2.75mm (C/2) hook and A, make 2ch.

Round 1 (RS): 10dc into 2nd ch, ss into first dc, turn. (10 dc)

Round 2: 1ch, 2dc into each dc, ss into first dc, turn. (20 dc)

Round 3: 1ch, [2dc into next dc, 1dc into next dc] to end, ss into first dc, turn. (30 dc)

Round 4: 1ch, 1dc into each dc, ss into first dc, turn.

Round 5: As Round 3. (45 dc)

Round 6: As Round 4.

Round 7: 1ch, [2dc into next dc, 1 dc into next 2dc] to end, ss into first dc, turn. (60 dc)

Rounds 8–9: As Round 4.

Round 10: 1ch, [2dc into next st, 1dc into 3dc] to end, ss into first dc, turn. (75 dc)

Round 11: As Round 4.

Round 12: 1ch, [2dc into next dc, 1dc into next 4dc] to end, ss into first dc, turn. (90 dc)

Rounds 13–16: As Round 4.

Round 17: 1ch, [2dc into next dc, 1dc into next 5dc] to end, ss into first dc, turn. (105 dc)

Rounds 18–23: As Round 4.

Round 24: 1ch, [2dc into next dc, 1dc into next 20dc] to end, ss into first dc, turn. (110 dc)

Rounds 25–34: As Round 4.
Change to 3.50mm (E/4) hook.

Rounds 35–39: As Round 4.

Round 40: 1ch, [2dc into next dc, 1dc into next 10dc] to end, ss into first dc, turn. (120 dc)

Rounds 41–42: As Round 4.

Round 43: 1ch, [2dc into next dc, 1dc into next 4dc] to end, ss into first dc, turn. (144 dc)

Rounds 44–48: As Round 4.

Round 49: 1ch, [2dc into next dc, 1dc into next 12dc] to end, ss into first dc, turn. (156 dc)

Rounds 50–52: As Round 4.

Work edging

With RS facing and using 2.75mm (C/2) hook and B, work 1 round of reverse dc into last round, ss into first dc.

Fasten off.

A floppy linen summer hat in pretty pastel colours, just perfect for lazy days in the sun

Materials
3 × 50g balls of Sirdar Organza, colour 287
4.50mm (G/6) crochet hook

Size
One size, to fit average adult head.

Tension
10 sts × 10 rows to 10cm (4in) with
4.50mm (G/6) hook.

Abbreviations
ch chain
dc double crochet
rtr raised treble
ss slip stitch
st(s) stitch(es)
tr treble

Note
The twists on the last round can be
graduated in size to appear longer at the
back or the sides – for each slight variation
just add 1ch to initial ch length of 5.

silky cloche hat

Dancing at teatime and early evening wearing beautiful silky
hats – the 'Bloomsbury set' enjoyed life to the full. This
evening-style cloche is reminiscent of Bloomsbury style and
the decorative edging mimics the tight curls peeping from
under ladies' hats. The shaping swirls around the head,
achieved by increasing at a certain point in the design.

Hat
Wrap the yarn around two fingers to
form a ring.

Round 1: 8dc in ring, pull ring tight,
ss to first dc.

Round 2: 1ch, 2dc into each dc, ss
into first dc. (16 dc)

Round 3: 1ch, [2dc in next dc, 1rtr
around stem of next dc] 8 times, ss
into first dc. (24 sts)

Round 4: 1ch, [1dc into each of 2dc,
1dc into rtr, 1rtr around stem of rtr
in round below] 8 times, ss into first
dc. (32 sts)

Round 5: 1ch, [1dc into each of 3dc,
1dc into rtr, 1rtr around stem of rtr
in round below] 8 times, ss into first
dc. (40 sts)

Round 6: 1ch, [1dc into each of 4dc,
1dc into rtr, 1rtr around stem of rtr
in round below] 8 times, ss into first
dc. (48 sts)

Round 7: 1ch, [1dc into each of 5dc,
1dc into rtr, 1rtr around stem of rtr
in round below] 8 times, ss into first
dc. (56 sts)

Round 8: 1ch, [miss 1dc into each of
5dc, 1dc in rtr, 1rtr around stem of
rtr in round below] 8 times, ss into
first dc. (56 sts)

Rounds 9–19: as Round 8.

Round 20: 3ch, [1tr into each dc to
rtr, 1tr into rtr, 5ch, miss first ch, 3dc
into each ch, ss into top of last tr] 8
times, ss into top of 3ch.
Fasten off.
Do not block.

*The decorative edging mirrors
the tight curls peeping from
under ladies' hats*

twizzle hat

The explosive cluster of twists at the crown of this hat and the riotous circus colours all demand attention! The inspiration for this design was the marvellous richness and clarity of the colours available in the yarn. You only need a tiny amount for each twist, so this is an ideal way to use up some of those left-over scraps.

Materials
1 x 100g ball of Wensleydale DK, pomegranate
Oddments of Wensleydale DK in eight different colours for corkscrew curls
3.50mm (E/4) crochet hook
5.50mm (I/9) crochet hook

Size
One size, to fit average adult head.

Tension
14 st x 22 rows to 5cm (2in) over dc worked into back loops on 5.50mm (I/9) hook.

Abbreviations
ch chain
dc double crochet
foll following
rep repeat
ss slip stitch
st(s) stitch(es)

Special abbreviations
dc2tog – double crochet two together, insert hook into next st, wrap yarn around hook, draw a loop through; rep this step into the next st (3 loops on the hook), wrap yarn and draw through all loops on the hook to complete.

HAT
Use yarn double throughout. Work in back loop only of each st.
Using 5.50mm (I/9) hook, make 2ch.
Round 1: 12dc in first ch, ss in first dc, 1ch, turn. (12 dc)
Round 2: 2dc in each st, ss in first dc, 1ch, turn. (24 dc)
Round 3: 1dc in each st, ss in first dc, 1ch, turn. (24 dc)
Round 4: *2dc in next st, 1dc in foll st; rep from *, ss in first dc, 1ch, turn. (36 dc)
Round 5: 1dc in each st, ss in first dc, 1ch, turn. (36 dc)
Round 6: *2dc in next st, 1dc in each of foll 2 sts; rep from *, ss in first dc, 1ch, turn. (48 dc)
Round 7: 1dc in each st, ss in first dc, 1ch, turn. (48 dc)
Round 8: *2dc in next st, 1dc in each of foll 3 sts; rep from *, ss in first dc, 1ch, turn. (60 dc)
Round 9: 1dc in each st, ss in first dc, 1ch, turn. (60 dc)
Round 10: *2dc in next st, 1dc in each of foll 4 sts; rep from *, ss in first dc, 1ch, turn. (72 dc)
Round 11: 1dc in each st, ss in first dc, 1ch, turn. (72 dc)
Round 12: *2dc in next st, 1dc in each of foll 5 sts; rep from *, ss in first dc, 1ch, turn. (84 dc)
Round 13: 1dc in each st, ss in first dc, 1ch, turn. (84 dc)

Round 14: *2dc in first st, 1dc in each of foll 6 sts; rep from *, ss in first dc, 1ch, turn. (96 dc)
Rounds 15–20: 1dc in each st, ss in first dc, 1ch, turn. (96 dc)
Round 21: *Dc2tog, 1dc in each of next 6 sts; rep from *, ss in first dc, 1ch, turn. (84 dc)
Round 22: *Dc2tog, 1dc in each of next 5 sts; rep from *, ss in first dc, 1ch, turn. (72 dc)
Rounds 23–31: 1dc in each st, ss in first dc, 1ch, turn. (72 dc)
Ribbing edge
Change to 3.50mm (E/4) hook.
Work ribbing in rows.
Row 2: Working in back loop only, 1dc in each of next 4sts, 1ch, turn.
Row 3: Working in back loop only, 1dc in each of next 4 sts, ss in each of next 2sts of last round of hat.
Rep Rows 2–3 around last row of hat. At end of last row of ribbing, working through back loop and opp side of foundation ch, ss in each of next 4 sts.

CORKSCREW CURLS
(make one in each shade)
Using 3.50mm (E/4) hook and yarn double, make 14ch, miss first ch, 4tr in each ch. Fasten off leaving a 10cm (4in) end. Sew to centre top of hat.

Materials
2 x 50g balls of Rowan Tapestry, colour 157
Moorland
12.00mm (P/16) crochet hook
4.00mm (G/6) crochet hook
Safety pin or contrast yarn for marker

Size
One size, to fit average adult head.

Tension
8¹/₂ sts to 10cm (4in) over treble, with
12.00mm (P/16) hook and using yarn
double (before fulling).

Abbreviations
ch chain
cont continue
dc double crochet
rep repeat
sp(s) space(s)
ss slip stitch
st(s) stitch(es)
tr treble

Special abbreviations
tr2tog – treble 2 together, leaving last
loop of each st on hook, work 1tr into
each of next 2tr, yarn around hook and
draw through all three loops..

cashmere helmet

The way the light interplayed with the fibre of this beautiful
yarn, creating highlights and shadows, inspired the design.
The hat is fulled by hand so the colours mingle and blend like
a distant hillside clothed in claret, greens and pale blue.

HELMET
Using yarn double and 12.00mm
(P/16) hook, 3ch, ss into first ch to
form a ring.
Round 1: 3ch, 11tr into ring, ss into
top of 3ch. (12 sts)
Round 2: 3ch, 1tr into same place as
ss, 2tr into each tr, ss into top of 3ch.
(24 sts)
Round 3: 3ch, 1tr into same place as
ss, [1tr into next tr, 2tr into next tr]
11 times, 1tr into last tr, ss into top
of 3ch. (36 sts)
Round 4: 3ch, 1tr into same place as
ss, [1tr into each of next 2tr, 2tr into
next tr] 11 times, 1tr into each of last
2tr, ss into top of 3ch. (48 sts)
Round 5: 3ch, 1tr into same place as
ss, [1tr into each of next 11tr, 2tr
into next tr] 3 times, 1tr into each of
last 11tr, ss into top of 3ch. (52 sts)
Cont, working into sps between tr.
Rounds 6–14: Ss into sp before first
tr, 3ch, 1tr into each sp, ss into top
of 3ch.
Right ear flap
First row: Ss into sp before first tr,
3ch, 2tr into next sp, 1tr into each of
next 7sps, 2tr into next sp, turn.
(12 sts)
Work 3 rows.
Work tr2tog at each end of next row.
(10 sts)
Work 2 rows.
Fasten off.

Miss 19 sps after right ear flap for
forehead, rejoin yarn to next sp and
work left ear flap to match right ear
flap.

FRILL
Using one strand of yarn and
4.00mm (G/6) hook, make a 12cm
(4³/₄in) length of ch.
Row 1: Miss 3ch, 3tr into single
strand of each ch, turn.
Row 2: 3dc into each st.

EDGING
Using one strand of yarn and
4.00mm (G/6) hook attach yarn at
centre back neck, [1dc into st, 3ch,
1dc into each of next 2 sts] all round
edge, ss into first dc.
Fasten off.

MAKING UP
Allow frill to ruffle up unevenly,
press and stitch onto side of helmet.
Wash by hand in warmer than
normal water and rub hard to full
the hat – not felt it.

bejewelled shrug

The colours of the seasons often play an important role in my designs. This shrug uses wonderful, warm autumnal hues inspired by the changing shades of the leaves with beads to represent the glistening early morning dew.

Materials
1 x 50g ball of Trendsetter Yarns Mohair, marmalade
11375 stitch'n'craft beads, mix of orange with lime lining and black
3.00mm (C/2) crochet hook
0.75mm (US 12) crochet hook

Size
Length 28cm (11½in) excluding edging; width 120cm (48in).

Tension
32tr to 10cm (4in) using 3.00mm (C/2) crochet hook.

Abbreviations
beg beginning
ch chain
ch sp chain space
dc double crochet
htr half treble
RS right side
tr treble
WS wrong side

SHRUG
Using 3.00mm (C/2) hook, make 90ch.
Row 1: Place marker at beg of row, 1tr into 4th ch from hook, [1tr into each ch] to end. (90 sts) Work 9 rows tr. Start arched mesh.
Row 11: 6ch, 1dc in 10th ch from hook, *5ch, miss 3ch, 1dc in next ch; rep from * to end, turn.
Row 12: 6ch, *1dc in next ch sp, 5ch; rep from * ending 1dc in last ch sp, 2ch, 1tr in 4th of 9ch, turn.
Row 13: 6ch, 1dc in first 5ch sp, *5ch, 1dc in next ch sp; rep from * to end, turn.
Row 14: As Row 12, ending 1tr in first of 6ch, turn. Start large mesh.
Row 15: 1tr in 6th ch from hook, *1ch, miss 1ch, 1tr in next ch; rep from * to end, turn.
Row 16: 4ch, miss first tr and 1ch, *1tr in next tr, 1ch, miss 1ch; rep from * ending 1tr in next ch, turn.
Rows 17–18: As Rows 15–16.
Row 19: 1tr in 8th ch from hook, *2ch, miss 2ch, 1tr in next ch; rep from * to end, turn.
Rows 20: 5ch, miss first tr and 2ch, *1tr in next tr, 2ch, miss 2ch; rep from * ending 1tr in next ch, turn.
Row 21: 1tr in 8th ch from hook, *2ch, miss 2ch, 1tr in next ch; rep from * to end, turn. Start decreasing.
Row 22: *1tr in next tr, miss 2ch, 1tr; rep from * to end.
Rep Row 22 six more times. 30ch.

CENTRE PANEL
Break yarn, rejoin to first of 90ch with RS facing to work in opp direction. Start arched mesh.
Row 1: 6ch, 1dc in 10th ch from hook, *5ch, miss 3ch, 1dc in next ch; rep from * to end, turn.
Row 2: 6ch, *1dc in next ch sp, 5ch; rep from* ending 1dc in last ch sp, 2ch, 1tr in 4th of 9ch, turn.
Row 3: 6ch, 1dc in first 5ch sp, *5ch, 1dc in next ch sp; rep from * to end, turn.
Row 4: As Row 2 ending 1tr in first of 6ch, turn.
Row 5–8: As Rows 1–4. Start large mesh.
Row 9: 1tr in 6th ch from hook, *1ch, miss 1ch, 1tr in next ch; rep from * to end, turn.
Row 10: 4ch, miss first tr and 1ch, *1tr in next tr, 1ch, miss 1ch; rep from * ending 1tr in next ch, turn. Rep Rows 9–10 six more times.
Rows 38–39: Work 30htr. Break yarn, thread approx 200 beads.
Rows 40–43: Work 4 rows htr with beaded yarn.
Rows 44–45: Work 30htr. Start large mesh.
Row 46–49: As Rows 9–10. Start arched mesh.
Row 70–77: As Rows 1–4. Cont in treble mesh on 90 sts.
Row 78: 1tr in 8th ch from hook,

*2ch, miss 2ch, 1tr in next ch; rep from * to end, turn.

Row 79: 5ch, miss first tr and 2ch, *1tr in next tr, 2ch, miss 2ch; rep from * ending 1tr in next ch, turn.

Row 80: As Row 78.
Start decreasing.

Row 81: *1tr in next tr, miss 2ch, 1tr; rep from * to end.
Rep Row 81 six more times. (30 ch)

NECK FRILL

Row 1: 1 tr in every ch between 2 markers.

Next row: 2tr in every tr.

Next row: 4tr in every tr.

Bead edges

Thread beads on yarn for final row and pull up as required, or thread yarn after finishing last row and catch the beads along edges of neck frill and wrist frills.

ROSES

(make 4)

Make 35ch. 1tr in each ch, gather up and stitch down.

MAKING UP

Using slip stitch, fasten roses on each sleeve between wrist and underarm.

hydrangea blues scarf

The beautiful shades of blue in a bowl of fading hydrangea heads inspired this design – and because the weather was turning colder it seemed appropriate to make a scarf. The pompoms reminded me of the shape of the rounded flower heads. Using the super large needle combined with the crochet hook was great fun.

Materials
2 x 50g balls of Rowan RY Classic Baby Alpaca colour 202, thistle (A)
2 x 50g balls of Rowan RY Classic Silk Wool colour 305, clay (B)
5.00mm (H/8) crochet hook
25mm (US 50) knitting needle
Pompom maker
Organza and satin ribbon to tone with yarn
Seed beads and large, light-weight bead
Fine sewing needle
Thread to match ribbon

Size
Length 96cm (38in) including pompoms.

Tension
20 sts to 10cm (4in) and 9 rows to 12cm (4³/₄in) over patt using 5.00mm (H/8) hook.

Abbreviations
ch chain
dc double crochet
ss slip stitch
yrh yarn round hook

PATTERN
Use 1 strand of A and 1 strand of B together throughout. Make 28ch.
Row 1: Sl loop onto knitting needle and remove hook, tighten yarn. Balance blunt end of needle on your lap with point facing upwards, miss first ch, [insert hook in next ch and draw loop through, sl loop onto needle and remove hook, tighten yarn to keep tension even] 27 times, turn. (28 loops on needle)
Row 2: Insert hook through first 4 loops and drop them off needle, yrh and draw loop through, yrh and draw through loop, work 4dc into this set of loops, [insert hook through next 4 loops and drop them off needle, work 4dc into this set of loops] 6 imes, turn. (28 dc)
Row 3: Working into back loops only work 1ss in each dc, turn.
Row 4: Sl loop onto needle and remove hook, tighten yarn, miss first ss, [insert hook into back loop of next ss and draw loop through, sl loop onto needle and remove hook, tighten yarn to keep tension even] 27 times, turn. (28 loops on needle)
Rep Rows 2–4 until scarf measures 91cm (36¹/₂in) from beginning, ending with a Row 4.

Next row: As Row 2 but work 2dc not 4 into each group of 4 loops. (14 dc)
Next row: As Row 3.
Next row: As Row 4 but work into 2nd ss then every alt ss to end. (8 loops on needle)
Next row: As Row 2 but work 2dc not 4 into each group of 4 loops. (4 dc)
Next row: As Row 3.
Fasten off.

POMPOMS
Make 6 pompoms in varying sizes, colours and yarn mixtures. Make chains of varying lengths to attach pompoms to straight end of scarf. Work one large pompom, including lengths of organza and satin ribbon with your yarn as you wrap it around the pompom maker. Using a fine needle and matching thread, stitch clusters of seed beads to the ends of the organza ribbon in the large pompom. Make a short length of ch and attach to shaped end of scarf. Thread a large bead then join on pompom.

attitude gloves

Lacy gloves with attitude – these stylish accessories will add drama and character to even the simplest outfit. The gold gloves shown here have cropped fingers with a row of glass beads set around the finger ends. The variation shown on page 41 is made in two shades of aqua, with full length fingers.

Materials

1 × 50g ball of Presencia Finca Perle cotton No 8, gold
1 × 50g ball of Presencia Finca Perle cotton No 8, aqua
1 × 50g ball of Presencia Finca Perle cotton No 8, dark aqua
1.50mm (No. 8 steel) crochet hook
Beads

Size

One size, to fit average adult hand.

Tension

The mesh stretches, so it is difficult to give a precise tension.

Abbreviations

beg beginning
ch chain
ch sp chain space
dc double crochet
dec decrease
foll following
inc increase
patt pattern
rep repeat
RS right side
ss slip stitch
st(s) stitch(es)

GLOVES

(Make 2)

Starting at the wrist, make 80ch, ss into first ch to make a ring.

Round 1: 5ch, miss 3ch, 1dc in next ch, [5ch, miss 3ch, 1dc in next ch] 20 times, ss into top of first 5ch arch at beg of round.

Round 2: 5ch, 1dc in next 5ch arch, [5ch, 1dc into next 5ch arch] 20 times, ss into top of first 5ch arch at beg of round.

Rep Round 2 until there are 20 rounds of ch arch.

Round 23: 30ch, skip 4ch arch, 1dc in next ch arch (this forms the opening for the thumb), work a row of ch arch, 5ch, miss 2sts of ch, dc in next st.

Round 24: *5ch, miss 4ch, 1dc in next st, rep from * 4 times, patt to end.

Round 25: 5ch, 1dc in next ch arch (there should be 21 ch arch in this row).

Rounds 26–33: Work 8 more rows as Row 2 and cont loops to left of thumb opening.

Fingers for full glove

Fold work with thumb opening at extreme left and work first finger directly over thumb.

Work 5ch arch over back of glove, 5ch, 1dc in 4th of 5ch arch on inside front of glove making 6 free 5ch arch for finger, work six 5ch arch, 5ch, 1dc in centre st of ch between fingers, 5ch, 1dc in next free 5ch arch. (5ch arch)

Cont working in patt in 5ch arch until there are 8 rounds for little finger and 10 rounds for a long finger, then work 4 rounds of 4ch arch, 2 rounds of 2ch arch, 2ch, 1dc in each 5ch arch, draw sts tog to close finger tip, fasten off.

Middle finger

Join thread to bottom of forefinger on back of glove, work three 5ch arch, 5ch, dc in 2nd of 5ch arch on inside of glove, work 1ch arch, 5ch, dc in first loop between fingers, 5ch, dc in loop between fingers, 5ch, dc in centre st of ch arch between fingers, 5ch, dc in next free ch. (7ch arch)

Lacy gloves with attitude will add drama and character to any outfit

Tips

● As you work the mesh design for these gloves you will be amazed to find that it has a slight elasticity, which is just perfect for these gloves. This is due to the yarn, so it will not be the same if you choose an alternative yarn to make the project.

● When choosing beads for use in knitting and crochet projects, buy from a reputable supplier. A size 6 is usually fine for crochet cotton – just make sure that the central hole is large enough so the yarn you are using will pass through easily. Glass beads are better than plastic, which may melt at high temperatures or if caught with an iron.

● Handwash these gloves as needed and dry flat.

● There are so many colours available in the Presencia yarn that you will be spoilt for choice!

Cont work until there are 10 rows. Work 6 rows of 4ch arch, 3 rows of 2ch arch and finish same as forefinger.

Ring finger

Work first 10 rows same as middle finger and then finish same as forefinger.

Little finger

Work 8 rows of 5ch arch and finish same as forefinger.

Thumb

Join thread to lower right side of opening and work twelve 5ch arch, work 3 more rows of 12 ch arch each.

Next row: Work three 5ch arch, dc in next loop omitting the ch between; rep from beg twice (dec 3 ch arch), work one row of ch arch.

Next row: Dec 2 ch arch on inside of thumb and work 1 more row of 5ch arch then work 4 rows of 8ch arch, 1dc in each ch arch and finish off same as fingers.

Fingers for cropped gloves

Work all fingers as for full glove, but length is determined by reaching first joint of middle finger.

Last row: 3ch, 1dc in next ch arch. Fasten off.

CUFFS

Thread beads onto yarn if desired and stitch around top edge of all fingers and thumb.

Full gloves

Change to a contrast colour and thread red beads onto yarn.

Rows 1–3: 5ch, dc in next 5ch arch. Change back to main colour.

Rows 4–5: 5ch, dc in next 5ch arch, placing beads as shown.

Fasten off.

Cropped gloves

Row 1: 5ch, 1dc in every other 5ch arch.

Row 2: 5ch, dc in every 5ch arch.

Fasten off.

Variations

The variation on this pattern above has completed fingers and also uses two different colours of yarn – the darker colour at the base accentuates the shape of the cuff a little more.

The beads around the ends of the cropped fingers must be omitted here, so for extra sparkle, you could work beads along the edge of the cuff instead – or even stitch sequins on after the gloves are finished.

Materials

3 x 50g balls of Twilleys Spirit, fire
4.00mm (F/5) crochet hook

Size

One size, to fit average adult head.

Tension

18 sts x 17 rows to 10cm (4in) over
pattern using 4.00mm (F/5) hook.

Abbreviations

ch chain
dc double crochet
dec decrease
htr half treble
inc increase
patt pattern
rep repeat
rem remain
RS right side
sp(s) space(s)
ss slip stitch
st(s) stitch(es)
tch turning chain
tr treble
WS wrong side

Special abbreviations

dc2tog – double crochet two together,
insert hook into next st, wrap yarn around
hook, draw a loop through; rep this step
into the next st (3 loops on the hook),
wrap yarn and draw through all loops on
the hook to complete.
dc3tog – double crochet three together,
insert hook into next st, wrap yarn around
hook, draw a loop through; rep this step
into the next st twice (3 loops on the
hook), wrap yarn and draw through all
loops on the hook to complete.

squared beret

Memories of a misty, murky Scottish morning in October led
to this design. I first created it in knitting, then translated the
pattern into crochet instead. After completing the crochet the
corners are pulled together and stitched to the edging band to
give the beret its billowing shape. The flower trim is made
separately and stitched onto the band as a finishing touch.

BERET

Make 27 ch.
Row 1: Miss 3ch (count as 1tr), [1dc
into next ch, 1tr into next ch] to end,
turn. (25 sts)
Row 2: 3ch (counts as 1tr), miss first
tr, [1dc into next dc, 1tr into next tr]
to end working last tr into top of
3ch, turn.
Row 3 (inc row): 1ch, [1dc, 1tr] into
first tr, [1dc into next dc, 1tr into
next tr] to end, ending 1dc into last
dc, [1tr, 1dc] into top of 3ch, turn.
(1 st inc at each end)
Row 4 (inc row): 3ch, 1dc into first
dc, [1tr into next tr, 1dc into next
dc] to end, ending 1tr into last tr,
[1dc, 1tr] into last dc, turn. (1 st inc
at each end)
Rep Rows 3–4 until there are 73 sts.
Place marker at each end of last row.
Now work straight, rep Row 2, until
work measures 29cm (11½in). Place
marker at each end of last row.
Next row: Ss into first tr and first dc,
1ch, 1dc into same dc, [1tr into next
tr, 1dc into next dc] to within tch,
turn. (1 st dec at each end)
Next row: Ss into first dc and first tr,
2ch, (count as first st), [1dc into next
dc, 1tr into next tr] to last 2 sts, 1htr
in last tr, turn. (1 st dec at each end)
Rep these last 2 rows until 25 sts
rem.

Work 2 rows straight working last tr
into top of 2ch on first row.
Fasten off.

BORDER

Starting at the centre of the lower
straight edge (the 27ch at the start),
work 1ch, 1dc into each base ch to
start of diagonal shaping, ignore this
shaping, work 25dc evenly along
next straight edge (between
markers), ignore next diagonal
shaping, 1dc into each 25 sts along
next top straight edge, ignore next
diagonal shaping, work 25dc evenly
along next straight edge (between
markers), ignore next diagonal
shaping, work 1dc into each of rem
base ch, ss into first dc, turn. (100
dc)
Next round: 1ch, 1dc into same
place as ss, 1dc into each dc, working
dc3tog into 3 sts at each corner, ss
into first dc, turn. (92 sts)
Next round: 1ch, work in dc, at same
time dec 2 sts evenly spaced along
each of the four sides, working each
dec as dc2tog, ss into first dc, turn.
(84 sts)
Next round: 1ch, 1dc into each st, ss
into first dc, turn.
Rep last round until border measures
7.5cm (3in), ending with a WS row.

Picot edging

With RS facing, work 1ch, [1dc, 3ch, 1dc] into first st, *miss next st, [1dc, 3ch, 1dc] into next st; rep from * to last st, 1dc into last st, ss into first dc. Fasten off.

FLOWER

Make 2ch.

Round 1: 20tr into first ch, ss into first tr to form a circle.

Round 2: Working into front loop only, 1ch, 1dc into same place as ss, 3ch, ss into top of dc, (picot made), *1dc into each of next 2tr, 3ch, ss into top of last dc, (picot made); rep from * ending 1dc into last tr, ss into first dc.

Round 3: Working into back loop only, ss into first back loop, 1ch, 1dc into same place as ss, 5ch, miss 3tr, *1dc into next tr, 5ch, miss 3tr; rep from * ending ss into first dc.

Round 4: Ss into ch sp, [1dc, 1htr, 3tr, 1htr, 1dc] into each ch sp (5 petals made), ss into first dc. Fasten off.

Round 5: Rejoin yarn to back loop of centre tr of a group of 3tr missed when working Round 3, 1dc into same place as ss, *7ch, 1dc into back of centre tr of next group of 3tr; rep from * to end, ss into first dc. (5 loops made)

Round 6: 1ch, [1dc, 1htr, 2tr, 3dtr, 2tr,1htr, 1dc] into each ch sp, ss into first dc. Fasten off.

MAKING UP

With WS of beret facing, sew the four corner seams using backstitch, or crochet together using dc. Turn beret back to RS.

Sew flower onto one side of hat on the border edging.

The pleated corners of the top give this beret its stylish billowing shape

Tips

● There are many different colours available in this yarn, so choose one to suit you. Look at it in daylight against your face before buying.

● The flower trim in the same yarn adds that 'certain something' to your hat. If a flower does not appeal to you, try a different design such as a curlicue or a bobble trim.

● The flower can also be made as a brooch to add to your outfit for a coordinated look. Try making the first round in black yarn – it makes the flower very eyecatching.

● When you make the trim and fasten off leave a long end, which you can use to sew the trim onto the beret securely. If you make alternative trims to match different outfits, for quick changes pin the trim to the beret with a safety pin rather than stitching in place.

jewellery

For me the process of making pieces to wear as jewellery – whether from wire, beads, felt, knitting or crochet – always starts with a memory invoked when I see a new yarn or a stone or bead. I had great fun creating these pieces, using recollections of things such as toffee sweets for the Toffee Drop Beads, or the subtle greys of my favourite dale in Yorkshire for the Dales Grey Necker. I also used bead crochet, which is not as popular as it should be, for the Speckled Brown Bracelet and its variations.

The opportunity to buy beautiful mineral stones created over hundreds of years, and to use them with a very modern concept in yarn, has given us an unusual Mosspath Bracelet and matching brooch. Using surplus beads and crochet cotton with the simplest of stitches, I have created the Spring Flowers Necklace and Meadow Time bracelet; these pieces are ideal to pack as holiday jewellery, leaving the precious metals and precious stones at home while you have fun in the sun.

I am always inspired by the colours of the seasons, so the projects in this chapter are bright and colourful. Make your own choices – nothing needs to be exactly as shown here!

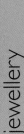

spring flowers necklace

Two-tone pink and spring-fresh green mix well – use up any spare beads that tone in this delightful necklace that matches the bracelet on page 51. Its inspiration was the same as the bracelet, but it is much softer in character and offers a great opportunity to use up all those odd accumulated beads.

Materials

1 10g × ball of Presencia Finca Perle cotton No 8, pale pink
1 10g × ball of Presencia Finca Perle cotton No 8, dark pink
1 10g × ball of Presencia Finca Perle cotton No 8, pale green
1 10g × ball of Presencia Finca Perle cotton No 8, gold
0.75mm (No. 12 steel) crochet hook
Size 6 pastel bead mix
Sewing needle

Size

One size.

Tension

Tension is not important for this project.

Abbreviations

bch bead chain
ch chain
ch sp chain space
dc double crochet
foll following
rep repeat
ss slip stitch
st(s) stitch(es)
tr treble

Special abbreviations

dc2tog – double crochet two stitches together; insert hook into next st, wrap yarn around hook, draw a loop through; rep this step into the next st (3 loops on the hook), wrap yarn and draw through all loops on the hook to complete.

Notes

Thread all the beads you will need onto each individual strand before commencing.

DEEP PINK STRING

Using the deeper pink cotton, 8ch, work 6ch, ss to 8th ch, go back and work 1tr in each st, 9ch, 1bch, 6ch, 1bch, 24ch, 1bch, 7ch, 1bch, 3ch, 7ch 1bch, 2ch, 1bch, [4ch 1tr in each st, 2bch, 3ch] ss back on itself, 1ch, 1bch, 12ch, 1bch, 18ch, 1bch, [4ch, 2tr in each st, 2bch, 8ch, 2bch, 9ch, 2bch, 10ch, 4ch, 1bch] ss back on itself, 12ch, 1bch, 8ch, 1bch 15ch, 1bch, 4ch, 1bch, [4ch, then 1tr in each of these 4ch, 2bch, 3ch] ss back on itself, 7ch, 2bch, 5ch, 2bch, 9ch, 1bch, 8ch, 1bch, 1bch, 1ch, 1bch, 5ch 1bch, 9ch, 1bch, 6ch, 1bch.
Attach to top of tab by dc across all sts and down one side. Fasten off and cut yarn leaving a 5cm (2in) long end. Thread this end on a needle and feed into work to close off.

PALE PINK STRING

Work this string similar to the deep pink string but attach the two together at intervals:
Using the paler pink cotton, 12ch, 1bch, 2ch, 1bch, 8ch, 1bch, attach I green flower on 2ch, 1bch, 6ch, attach to deeper pink string with dc, 11ch, 2bch, 11ch, 1bch, 3ch, 2bch, 3ch, 1bch, 7ch, 1bch 12ch, attach to deeper pink string with dc, 8ch, 1bch, 4ch, 2bch, 3ch, ss back on

itself, 4ch, 2bch, 9ch, 2bch, 11ch, loop of 6ch, 1bch, 3ch, 1bch, 13ch, 1bch, 14ch, 1bch, 18ch, 1bch, 4ch, 2bch, 3ch, ss back on itself, attach to deeper pink string with dc, 11ch, 1bch, 5ch, 1bch, 3ch, 1bch, attach to deeper pink string with dc, 5ch, 1bch, 5ch, 1bch, 3ch, 1bch, attach to tab fastener.

GREEN STRING

Make 1 leaf: 6ch, 1tr in each of 5ch, 1dc in 6th ch, turn.
Next Row: 1dc, 5tr, 7ch, loop of 5ch, 7ch, loop 6ch, 30ch, loop 8ch, 6ch, attach 1 green flower, 8ch, 1bch, 5ch, 1bch, 6ch, 1bch, 22ch, 1bch, 3ch, 2bch, 12ch, 1bch, 3ch, 1bch, 6ch, 1bch, 6ch, make loop of 16ch, 1bch, make leaf, 11ch, 3bch, 9ch, 1bch, 5ch, 2bch, attach 1 green flower, 15ch.
Wind around the two pink strings and attach to tab fastener.

CLOSURE LOOP

Take the ends of the two pink strings and make 3 loops of 8ch each and attach together.
Tab fastener
Row 1: 3ch, 1tr in each st, 1ch. (6 sts)
Row 2: 2tr in each st. (12 sts)
Row 3: 1tr in each st. (12 sts)
Row 4: 2tr in each st. (24 sts)

Row 5: 1tr in each st. (24 sts)
Reverse shaping for next 5 rows and,
holding both sides together, change
thread to pale gold.
Row 1: Dc in each st.

Row 2: Dc2tog in every st.
Rows 3–7: Dc in each st.
Attach a bead on the end for weight.
Thread through loops for fastening.

For steps to make flower petals, see
next page.

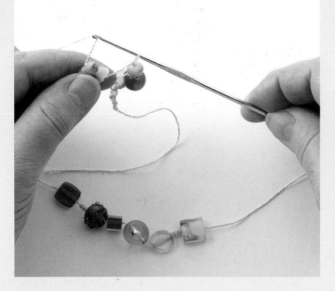

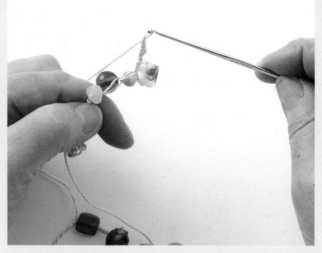

1. Make slip knot in the yarn. Make another slip knot, bringing the bead up and catching it inside the slip knot.

2. Make five chain stitches in the yarn, to create a length of chain after the bead.

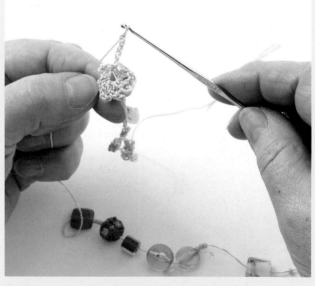

3. Return to the first chain and make a slip knot to join the chain into a ring.

4. Repeat the last three steps four times more to make five flower petals.

meadow time

Soft summer greens, pale and dark pink sweet peas, memories past... all went into the design of this cool-to-wear bracelet for those hot, hot summer days. The necklace on page 48 is ideal to wear with this if you make it in the same colours.

Materials
1 10g × ball of Presencia Finca Perle cotton No 8 pale pink
1 10g × ball of Presencia Finca Perle cotton No 8 dark pink
1 10g × ball of Presencia Finca Perle cotton No 8 pale green
0.75mm (No. 12 steel) crochet hook
Size 6 pastel bead mix in pink and green

Size
19 × 7cm (7^1/$_2$ × 2^3/$_4$in).

Tension
Each ring measures 3.5cm (1^3/$_8$in).

Abbreviations
ch chain
dc double crochet
ss slip stitch
st(s) stitch(es)

Notes
There are 3 parts to this bracelet: the circles; the tabs that hold them; and the flowers that form the fasteners.

CIRCLES

(Make 5 dark pink and 5 pale pink)
Wind a length of pink cotton around
two fingers 9 times, then work 45dc
into this circle, ss into first dc.
Fasten off.

TABS

(Make 12 in green)
Make 13ch.
Row 1: 1dc into 2nd ch from hook,
1dc into each ch, turn.
Row 2: 1ch, 1dc into each dc to end,
turn.
Row 3: As Row 2.
Fasten off.

FLOWER FASTENER

First side
Round 1: Wind the green cotton
around two fingers 9 times, then
work 45dc into this circle, ss into
first dc.

Round 2: [10ch, miss next dc, ss into
front loop of next dc] to end, ss into
first ch.
Round 3: [Ss into front loop of
missed dc, 10ch] to end, ss into
first ss.
Fasten off.
Second side
With green, make 46ch.
Round 1: 1ss into 2nd ch from hook,
[10ch, miss 1ch, 1dc into next ch] to
end.
Row 2: [10ch, 1ss into missed ch] to
end.
Fasten off.

MAKING UP

Alternating colours, lay out circles in
2 rows of 5. Wrap a tab around
adjoining circles and join with dc as
illustrated below. Sew first side of
flower fastener to one end of
bracelet. Fold second side of flower
fastener in half and sew along ch
edge. Sew to other end of bracelet.
Stitch a small cluster of seed beads
on flower fastener.

1. To join the chain, lay two chain links down next to one
another, with a green tab placed over the top.

2. With the crochet hook, pick up two stitches on either side
of the green tab and join with double crochet.

speckled brown bracelet

Bead crochet is not often made today, but you can use it to make the most wonderful chunky jewellery. These pieces were initially inspired by the thick clusters of little round flowers on the grape hyacinths in my garden.

Materials
1 10g × ball of Presencia Finca Perle cotton No 8, beige
0.75mm (No. 12 steel) crochet hook
Size 6 bead mix

Size
One size, to fit average adult wrist.

Tension
Just make sure the beads are thickly clustered together.

Abbreviations
ch chain
ss slip stitch
st(s) stitch(es)

Notes
To yield 2.5cm (1in) of 5 around beads in size 6 you will need to thread 14cm (5½in). Bead crochet patterns are shown as tables of sequences and for the first bracelet you simply have a 5 bead repeat. To check you are doing the beading correctly, you should see the beads you are yet to do lying sideways and the beads you have done lying upwards.

BRACELET

Make a rope of beads for the bracelet following the illustrated steps for bead crochet on pages 56–57.

MAKING UP

Stitch one half of a fastener onto each end of the rope.

Continued on next page.

Notes

The top picture opposite shows how the bracelet will look if the beads are initially threaded in a totally random order.

The ginger and black beads bracelet below illustrates what happens when you follow a pattern – these beads were threaded on in a sequence of:
4,2,4,2,4,2,4,2,4,2,4,2.

For matching earrings, see page 58. They are made in exactly the same way, but as drops attached to earring backs.

Try making a necklace too – the principle is exactly the same as the bracelet, you just need more beads!

1. The perle cotton used for this project is very fine and thin, but before you purchase your beads make sure the central hole is large enough to take the thread.

2. Start by threading your beads onto the yarn. If you thread the colours in order it gives a different effect to threading them randomly (see photos of alternative effects on page 55).

3. The thread comes over the index finger, which gives you tension. Make a slip knot in the end of your thread leaving a 20cm (8in) tail.

4. Chain 6, leaving one bead in each stitch.

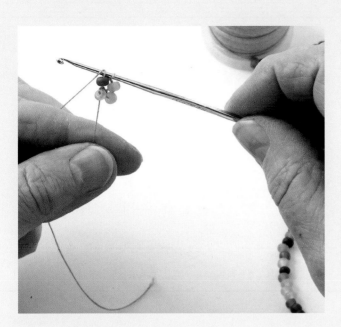

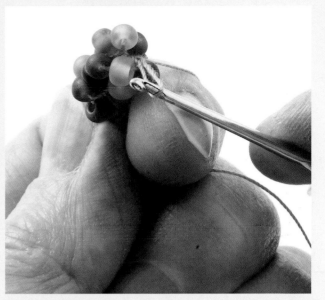

5. Pull up the row of beads to form a curve; you are aiming to get the beads on the outside. Join the chain to the first stitch with a slip stitch.

6. Flip the bead over the to the right and hold down tightly. Visually flicking the bead over is important so the bead lies to the outside and the thread to the inside.

7. Pull down the next bead and catch the thread above it.

8. Pull the thread through the first loop on the hook. Pull this loop through the 2nd loop on yarn. This gives you one stitch with a bead.

variations

pink and white bracelet

The pink version of the Speckled Brown Bracelet on page 54 uses toning shades of pink beads for a subtle effect.

Follow the illustrated steps for bead crochet on pages 56–57 to make this bracelet. Here again, the beads are initially threaded on in a random order.

metallic earrings

Metallic beads are very effective for this type of work, and you can also use flattened beads, as here, rather than perfectly round ones.

When making the earrings, thread the loose ends of the yarn at the dangling end of the earrings up inside the beads at the end, before trimming them off. This will give your earrings a neater and more professional finish.

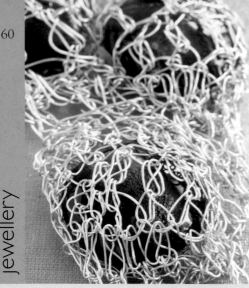

toffee drop beads

A recollection of the wonderful array of differing toffees that were available when I was a child inspired this crocheted bracelet. Each luscious bead is trapped inside a cell of champagne-coloured wire – sounds good enough to eat.

Materials
1 × reel of 0.315mm champagne wire
2.00mm (B/1) crochet hook
6 × toffee drop glass beads from Injabulo
1 decorative clasp

Size
One size, to fit average adult wrist.

Tension
Tension is not important on this project.

Abbreviations
ch chain
ch sp chain space
dc double crochet
rep repeat
ss slip stitch
st(s) stitch(es)
tch turning chain

BRACELET

Leaving a 10cm (4in) tail, make 12ch.
Row 1: Ch1, dc into 4th ch from hook, 1dc in each ch sp.
Row 2: 2tch, 1dc into each front loop of previous row.
Rows 3–4: As Row 2.
Enclose each glass piece within its own little wire cell and fasten the three sides by using the wire as stitching thread and working an overhand stitch. See page 62 for illustrated steps.

MAKING UP

Place the pieces in two staggered rows and join the cells up with small crocheted links. See page 62 for illustrated steps.

LINKS

Row 1: Insert hook into top of wire cell, 3dc across top.
Row 2: 2tch, 1dc in each space.
Close off through top loops and bottom loops of next cell, using ss as shown in step 4 on page 62.
Attach clasp using fine wire to stitch onto either end.

Continued on the next page.

Luscious toffee-colour beads trapped in a delicate cage of fine wire look good enough to eat

1. Place a stone on top of one square of mesh. Fold the mesh around the stone.

2. Join the open sides by 'stitching' with wire.

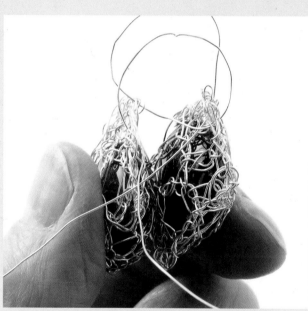

3. Close off the links through the top loops and bottom loops of the next cell, using slip stitch as shown

quick crochet

mosspath bracelet

Some time ago I studied moss and lichen for a textile exam, and it inspired this bracelet – as well as working with this amazing yarn. See also the brooch variation of this bracelet shown on page 65.

MATERIALS
1 × 50g balls of NoroGanpi Abaka Surabu, colour 62
1.75mm (No. 6 steel) crochet hook
2 × mineral agate disks with central hole

SIZE
One size, to fit average adult wrist.

TENSION
Just make sure the beads are thickly clustered together.

ABBREVIATIONS
ch chain
ch sp chain space
dc double crochet
ss slip stitch
st(s) stitch(es)
tr treble

Continued on the next page.

RECTANGLE
(Make 3)
Make 5ch, ss in first ch to form a ring.
Round 1: 1ch, [1dc into ring, 2ch, 2dc into ring] 4 times, ss into first dc.
Round 2: Ss into 2ch sp, 3ch, 2tr into same 2ch sp, 5ch, 3dc into next 2ch sp, 5ch, 3tr into next 2ch sp, 5ch, 3dc into next 2ch sp, 5ch, ss into top of 3ch.

Round 3: Working into back loop of each st, work 1dc into each st, working 2dc into centre of 5ch at each corner. Fasten off.

MAKING UP
Using a sewing needle and Noro yarn, stitch the mineral pieces to the yarn pieces as shown. Attach clasp to the end of the mineral stones.

NOTES
The bracelet consists of three identical rectangles with differing stone rings placed in between, as shown in the picture.
Take care not to wet too much.

1. The rectangles are worked mainly in double crochet: insert the hook under the second chain from hook, yarn round hook and pull through, yarn around again and pull through remaining two loops on hook.

2. With treble crochet, yarn round hook, insert hook under fourth chain from hook, yarn round and pull one loop through, yarn round, draw through first two loops on hook, yarn round again and pull through remaining two loops on hook.

3. To add the stone rings to the bracelet, thread the end of the yarn through the centre of the ring to attach it to the crochet as shown.

4. For the brooch variation, sew the stone ring to the centre of the crochet sqaure with evenly-spaced stitches around the entire ring.

The matching brooch is made with four rectangles joined in a 'flower' shape as shown above – although you could arrange them differently if you prefer. Stitch one of the mineral rings into the centre of the brooch for added interest and to introduce an attractive contrast in texture.

The wonderful Noro yarn that is used for this project includes paper fibre in its composition, so take care not to get the jewellery too wet when you are wearing it.

A matching necklace is very simple to make – just follow the instructions for the bracelet but make more rectangles. Remember that you will also need more yarn and more mineral rings for the necklace than are specified for the bracelet.

Materials
1 x 10g ball of Presencia Finca Perle cotton No 08
2.00mm (B/1) crochet hook
Approx 200 irregular glass beads in assorted colours, shapes and sizes
2 springs
2 crimp beads
2 end connectors with 3/1 holes
Short length of chain
Lobster clasp

Size
One size, to fit average adult wrist.

Tension
Just make sure the beads are thickly clustered together.

Abbreviations
ch   chain
rep   repeat

summer extravaganza bracelet

This glorious bracelet is made of a rich cluster of brightly-coloured irregular glass beads. The strange shapes of the beads add a random texture to the piece.

1. Make 1ch, slide 3 beads up to hook.

2. Take hook to far side of 3 beads, 1ch.

3. At the end, put on a spring – this stops the cotton fraying.

4. Add a silver crimp bead after the spring with pliers as shown.

5. Thread the spare end of the yarn through the clasp.

6. Stitch the thread onto the clasp with a backstitch. Add a drop of glue to keep the clasp firmly fixed.

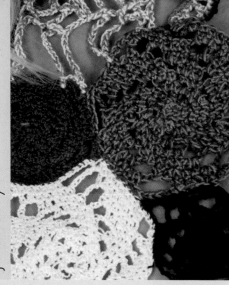

Materials

1 x 50g ball of Presencia Finca Perle cotton
No 8, colour 0007, black
1 x 50g ball of Presencia Finca Perle cotton
No 8, colour 8742, taupe
1 x 50g ball of Presencia Finca Perle cotton
No 8, colour 8756, dark grey
1 x 50g ball of Presencia Finca Perle cotton
No 8, colour 8767, silver grey
1 x 50g ball of Twilleys Crochet cotton,
silky white
2.00mm (B/1) crochet hook
4 buttons

Size

This is worked as a continuous spiral so the
size can be whatever you wish.

Tension

Tension is not important on this project.

Abbreviations

ch chain
cont continue
dc double crochet
dtr double treble
patt pattern
rep repeat
RS right side
ss slip stitch
st(s) stitch(es)
tog together
tr treble

Notes

Make four spirals, two large (approx 9cm
(3¹/₂in)) and two medium (approx 5.5cm
(2¹/₄in)), with one black, one white, one
dark grey and one dark grey and taupe
together.

dales grey necklet

This dramatic necklet is made of four crochet circles in
different sizes and shades, which are linked and then fastened
by an attached mesh collar trimmed with a border of double
crochet in a contrasting yarn.

SPIRALS

Make 2ch, work 6tr into 2nd ch from
hook, ss into first tr.
Cont as foll until spiral is chosen size:
1ch, work 1tr into same st as ss, 3ch,
[1tr into next tr, 3ch] 5 times, [1tr
into next tr, 1tr into next sp, 3ch] 6
times, [miss 1tr, 1tr into next tr, 2tr
into next sp, 3ch] 6 times, [miss 1tr,
1tr into each of next 2tr, 2tr into
next sp, 4ch] 6 times, [miss 1tr, 1tr
into each of next 3tr, 2tr into next
4ch sp, 4ch] 6 times, [miss 1tr, 1tr
into each of next 4tr, 2tr into next
4ch sp, 5ch] 6 times, [miss 1tr, 1tr
into each of next 5tr, 2tr into next
5ch sp, 5ch] 6 times, [miss 1tr, 1tr
into each of next 6tr, 2tr into next
5ch sp, 6ch] 6 times, [miss 1tr, 1tr
into each of next 7tr, 2tr into next
6ch sp, 6ch] 6 times, [miss 1tr, 1tr
into each of next 8tr, 2tr into next
6ch sp, 7 ch] 6 times.
Fasten off when size is achieved.
Sew spirals tog as in photograph.

MESH COLLAR

Using silver grey make 18ch.
Buttonhole row: 1dc into 2nd ch
from hook, [3ch, miss 3ch, 1dc into
next ch] 4 times, turn.
Cont in patt:
Row 1: 7ch, miss first dc, [1dtr into
next dc, 3ch] 3 times, 1dtr into last
dc, turn.
Row 2: 7ch, miss first dtr, [1dtr into
next dtr, 3ch] 3 times, 1dtr into 4th
of 7ch, turn.

Rep Row 2 until band measures
16cm (6¹/₄in). Cont in patt joining
band to spirals:
Row 1: Patt to end, 12ch, 1dc into
corner of top left-hand spiral, turn.
Row 2: 12ch, 1dtr into dtr, patt to
end.
Row 3: Patt to end, 10ch, 1dc into
opp corner of same spiral, 3ch, 1dc
into same spiral a few sts from last
dc, turn.
Row 4: 10ch, 1dtr into next dtr, patt
to end.
Spread next 4 joins irregularly along
top right-hand spiral.
Row 5: Patt to end, 8ch, 1dc into
corner of spiral, turn.
Row 6: 8ch, 1dtr into dtr, patt to end.
Row 7: Patt to end, 6ch, 1dc into
spiral, 1ch, 1dc into spiral, turn.
Row 8: 6ch, 1dtr into dtr, patt to end.
Row 9: Patt to end, **10ch, 1dc into
spiral, turn.
Row 10: 1ch, miss 1ch, [1tr into next
ch, 2ch, miss 2ch] 3 times, 1dtr into
next dtr, patt to end.
Patt 2 rows.
Rows 13 and 14: As Rows 9 and 10.
Patt until band fits quite tightly
around neck.
Next row: 1dc into each st, turn.
Work 3 rows dc for button band.
Fasten off.
With RS facing, join black to Row 9
of band at point marked **. Work dc
around outer edge of band, ending at
point where Row 1 joins first spiral.
Fasten off and sew on buttons.

accessories

These accessories have been a marvellous opportunity to work with yarn on a range of smaller items. They are all part of a collection of designs dreamt up after seeing exciting new yarns and deciding to run with them.

The projects in this chapter include a great selection of unusual and eyecatching bags, cushions that will not squash down, a chunky diary cover for him – and a fluffy one for her as well. The Travel Slippers and Hot Water Bottle Cover are perfect for luxurious moments when you are far away from home. And the cute little Pixie Purse can be whatever you want it to be: a small change purse; a lipstick-only bag; or lent to your favourite little daughter for those 'grown up' moments.

Whatever you choose to make, I hope you will enjoy the creative process as much as I have enjoyed designing all these great new projects.

Materials

3 × 50g balls of Patons Inca colour 7006,
green grey
6.00mm (J/10) crochet hook
5cm (2in) diameter button

Size

To fit diaries: 15cm (6in) wide × 21cm
(8 1/2in) deep.

Tension

11 sts × 12 rows to 5cm (2in) square over
pattern, using 6.00mm (J/10) hook.

Abbreviations

ch chain
ch sp chain space
dc double crochet
rep repeat
RS right side
st(s) stitch(es)
tr treble

Special abbreviations

1tr/rf – work 1tr around stem of next st
2 rows below, inserting hook around stem
from right to left to draw up loop.

his diary cover

This chunky diary cover in a masculine natural green-grey
yarn is just perfect for the men. The big wooden button is fine
for male hands – no fiddly little catches to deal with here! The
cover is designed to fit a standard size of diary, but check the
dimensions before you begin – it's easy to adjust the size as
you work if you need a bigger or smaller cover.

HIS DIARY COVER

Using 6.00mm (J/10) hook, make
55ch.

Row 1 (RS): 1 dc into 2nd ch from
hook, 1dc into each ch to end, turn.
(53 dc)

Row 2: 1ch, 1dc into each dc to
end, turn.

Row 3: 1 ch, 1dc into each of first
2dc, *1tr/rf round next dc 2 rows
below, 1dc into each of next 2dc; rep
from * to end, turn.

Row 4: 1ch, 1dc into each st to
end, turn.

Row 5: 1ch, 1dc into each of first
2dc, *1tr/rf around stem of next
tr/rf 2 rows below, 1dc into each of
next 2 dc; rep from * to end, turn.
Rep Rows 4 and 5 until work
measures 22cm (8 3/4in).
Fasten off.

STRAP

Using 6.00mm (J/10) hook, make
7ch.

Row 1: 1dc into 2nd ch from hook,
1dc into each ch to end, turn. (6 dc)

Row 2: 1ch, 1dc into each dc to end,
turn.

Rep Row 2 until strap is long enough
to stretch around diary, approx 36cm
(14in).

Next row (buttonhole row): 1ch,
1dc into first 2dc, 2ch, miss 2dc, 1dc
into each of next 2dc, turn.

Next row: 1ch, 1dc into first 2dc,
2dc into 2ch space, 1dc into next
2dc, turn.

Work a further 4 rows of dc as set.
Fasten off.

MAKING UP

Leaving 7.5cm (3in) for flap, fold
remainder of width over and join
both sides. Sew the button to front
with its centre 5cm (2in) from folded
edge. Sew strap to back 5cm (2in)
from fold with long end facing
towards flap.

A chunky diary cover in a cool green grey with a big wooden button – no fiddly little catches to deal with here

her diary cover

This fluffy marble diary cover with its big rose button fastener couldn't be more feminine, but if this is not your colour the yarn is available in a variety of other shades. Always try and find the perfect button for your project, or create one with beads or crochet – finishing touches like this do make a big difference to the final look.

Materials
3 x 50g balls of Anny Blatt Vega colour 368, marble
4.50mm (G/6) crochet hook
5cm (2in) rose button

Size
To fit diaries: 15cm (6in) wide x 21cm (8½in) deep.

Tension
7tr x 3 rows to 5cm (2in) square over pattern, using 4.50mm (G/6) hook.

Abbreviations
ch chain
ch sp chain space
dc double crochet
foll following
rep repeat
RS right side
st(s) stitch(es)
tr treble
WS wrong side

HER DIARY COVER

Using 4.50mm (G/6) hook, make 65ch.
Row 1 (RS): 1tr into 4th ch from hook, 1tr into each ch to end. (63 tr)
Row 2: 3ch, 1tr into each tr to end, working into back loop only, 1tr into top of 3ch, turn.
Row 3: 3ch, 1tr into each tr to end, working into front loop only, 1tr into top of 3ch, turn.
Rep Rows 2 and 3 until the work measures 22cm (8¾in).
Fasten off.

STRAP

Using 4.50mm (G/6) hook and B, make 7ch.
Row 1: 1dc into 2nd ch from hook, 1dc into each ch to end. (6 dc)
Row 2: 1ch, 1dc into each dc to end, turn.

Rep Row 2 until strap is long enough to stretch around diary, approx 36cm (14in).
Next row (buttonhole row): 1ch, 1dc into first 2dc, 2ch, miss 2dc, 1dc into each of next 2dc, turn.
Next row: 1ch, 1dc into first 2dc, 2dc into 2ch sp, 1dc into next 2dc, turn.
Work 6 rows dc.
Fasten off.

MAKING UP

Leaving 11cm (4¼in) for flap, fold remainder of width over and join both sides. Sew end of strap on back 5cm (2in) from folded edge, with long end of strap facing away from flap. Sew the button on back above strap.

Fluffy yarn makes a super-feminine diary cover – just the thing to bring a bit of romance into your life

felted weekend tote

The tote is 'this year's' bag and when I saw this yarn, I designed the bag for it – which is opposite to how I normally work, but I was really excited by the possibilities. This bag will take you from shopping to weekends away.

Materials
6 × 50g balls of Karaoke, red multi
4.00mm (F/5) crochet hook
3.50mm (E/4) crochet hook

Size
After felting: 34cm (13½in) wide; 30cm (12in) deep, excluding handles.
Before felting: 49cm (19½in) wide; 46cm (18½in) deep.

Tension
16tr × 8 rows to 10cm (4in) over treble using 3.50mm (E/4) hook, before felting.

Abbreviations
ch chain
dc double crochet
rep repeat
RS right side
ss slip stitch
st(s) stitch(es)
tr treble
WS wrong side

Special abbreviations
tr2tog – treble 2 together, wrap yarn around hook, insert hook into next st, wrap yarn around hook, draw a loop through, wrap yarn and draw through 2 loops on hook, (2 loops left on hook), rep into next st, (3 loops on hook), wrap yarn and draw through 3 loops on hook to complete.

BAG

(worked as one piece)
Using 4.00mm (F/5) hook, make 176ch, join with ss into first ch to form a circle. Change to 3.50mm (E/4) hook.
Round 1 (RS): 3ch, (count as first st), 1tr into each ch to end, ss into top of 3ch. (176 sts)
Round 2: 3ch, (count as first st), 1tr into each tr to end, ss into top of 3ch.
Rep this last round until work measures 32cm (13in).
Divide for handles.
Row 1: **2ch, miss first st, 1tr into next st (this counts as tr2tog), 1tr into each of next 17tr, tr2tog over next 2sts, turn. (19 sts)
Row 2: 1ch, 1dc into first st, 1tr into each of next 18 sts, turn. (19 sts)
Rep this last row a further 13 times. Fasten off. **
Miss next 37tr, rejoin yarn with a sl st into next st, repeat from ** to **.
Miss next 9tr, rejoin yarn with a sl st into next st, repeat from ** to **.
Miss next 37tr, rejoin yarn with a sl st into next st, repeat from ** to **.
9tr left unworked.

MAKING UP

With RS of bag facing, fold each handle in half lengthways, continuing to fold to lower edge of bag, pin together (this makes it easier to crochet together). To form folds at either side of bag, still with RS facing, using 4.00mm (F/5) hook and working through all 4 thicknesses, join top of 1st and 4th handles together by working 1 row of dc across folded handles. Fasten off. Join other 2 handles. Working through all 4 thicknesses at each end, and double thickness at centre, work 1 row of dc across lower edge of bag. Fasten off.

FELTING

To felt the bag, wear rubber gloves. Fill a bowl with hot water and put the bag into it. Leave for 10 mins, allowing the fibres to soak up the hot water. Add a little soap powder and stir around, dissolving the powder. Empty out some of the water and top up again with hot water; some dye may come out of the yarn, but do not worry. Squeeze and pummel the bag repeatedly so the yarn gets fluffier. Take the bag out occasionally and squeeze out excess water. Lay it flat and measure. If it is still too big, repeat the process again. When you have finished felting, put the bag into cold water and squeeze gently, then put it into a washing machine on a short spin cycle. Take out bag and pull back into shape, if needed. Place onto a towel and dry.

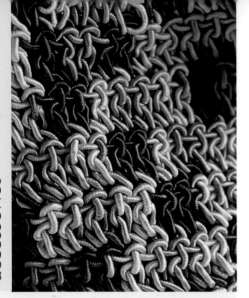

pixie purse

The smallest bag – a fun bag for the loose change in your main bag, or how about just a lipstick and credit card when you go out dancing! The delicious yarns available today just cry out to be bought and worked into something, but often it's a problem to find something to make with just one hank or ball. Well here is Pixie, a delight to suit any age group and to show off that chosen yarn to perfection.

Materials

1 x 50g hank of Noro Daria, colour 6
2.00mm (B/1) crochet hook
1 x 7.5cm (3in) purse frame from www.u-handbag.com
Fabric glue

Size

Width 10cm (4in); depth 8cm (3¹/4in).

Tension

20 sts x 9 rows to 10cm (4in) using 2.00mm (B/1) crochet hook.

Abbreviations

ch chain
RS right side
ss slip stitch
st(s) stitch(es)
tr treble
WS wrong side
yrh yarn round hook

Special abbreviations

tr2tog – treble 2 together, wrap yarn around hook, insert hook into next st, wrap yarn around hook, draw loop through, wrap yarn and draw through 2 loops on hook (2 loops left on hook); rep this step into next st (3 loops on hook), wrap yarn and draw through 3 loops on hook.

PURSE

Make 54ch. Worked with WS facing. Work into back loop of each st throughout.

Round 1: 2ch, 1tr into each ch, ss in top of 2ch.

Round 2: 2ch, 1tr into each tr, ss into top of 2ch.

Rep last round 4 times.

Round 7: 3ch, 1tr into each of next 3tr, tr2tog, [4tr, tr2tog] to end, ss in top of 2ch. (45 sts)

Fasten off.

Base

Rejoin yarn to first ch of foundation ch, 2ch, 1tr into each of next 17ch, turn. (18 sts)

Work 4 rows in tr.

Fasten off.

MAKING UP

Sew base in place. Turn the entire bag to RS.

Place 7.5cm (3in) purse frame into bag, with short side tops into the slits under the clasp and the hinged side fitting outside the sides.

Using fabric glue, coat both sides of the work and glue into frame groove. Push into place and hold for a few minutes, then place in cool place to dry firm.

Tips

● Using a purchased frame like the one in this project is an ideal way to make your finished item look professional. There is a wide range of types available from craft or yarn stores – or you can try the internet.

● The look of this purse can be changed by using a different frame, some of which have optional long chains so you can use the purse as a tiny shoulder bag.

● If you don't want to use glue to attach the purse to the frame, make sure you buy a frame with holes for stitching.

*The Pixie Purse is perfect
for life's little essentials*

bramble bag

A small wild bramble found giving forth its fruit in late summer – picked and eaten with fresh pouring cream – was the starting point for this design. The shape was taken from the wide base of the bramble, which narrowed as it climbed to find the sun for its fruits. The button is, of course, the largest bramble – which is always out of reach. A fun design to remind me of summer.

Materials
2 × 50g balls of
Louisa Harding Impressions, colour 06
1 large button
3.00mm (C/2) crochet hook

Size
Width 22cm (8¹/₂in); depth 15cm (6in)

Tension
20dc to 10cm (4in) on 3.00mm (C/2) hook.

Abbreviations
dc double crochet
tr treble
yrh yarn around hook

Special abbreviations
dc2tog – insert hook into next st, yrh, draw a loop through; rep into the next st, yrh, draw through all loops on hook.
tr2tog – yrh, insert hook into next st, yrh, draw a loop through, yrh, draw through 2 loops on hook; rep into next st, yrh, draw through all loops on hook.

FRONT
Make 46ch.
Row 1: 1dc into 2nd ch from hook, 1dc into each ch to end. (45 dc)
Row 2: 1ch, 1dc into first dc, dc2tog, 1dc into each dc to end.
Rep last row unil 23 sts remain. Cont straight until work measures 12cm (4³/₄in).
Fasten off.

BACK
Work as front but do not fasten off.

FLAP
Row 1: 3ch (counts as first tr), miss first st, tr2tog, 1tr into each st to last 3 sts, tr2tog, 1tr into last st, turn.
Rep last row until 5 sts remain.
Next row: 3ch, [tr2tog] twice, turn.
Next row: 2ch, tr2tog, yrh and drawn through 2 loops. Work a 30cm (12in) length of ch on remaining loop.
Fasten off.

STRAP
Make 4ch, ss into first ch to form a ring. Work 5dc into ring, then work in continuous rounds of dc until strap measures 35cm (14in).
Fasten off.

MAKING UP
Join sides of bag. Work ch loops along lower edge. [10ch, ss into each of next 2 sts] all around, varying no of ch in loops.
Fasten off.
Turn bag inside out and join lower straight edge leaving ch loops free. Turn to RS. Stitch the strap to the bag, making coil at one side to form a small circle.
Stitch large button to front using length of ch at end of flap to fasten bag.

Inspired by a late-fruiting bramble, this is a fun design to remind me of the summer

bobble bag

Think of hazy summer days, the soft green fields in the sun, lazy evenings – the textures and colours in this little bag bring back these wonderful memories.

Materials

1 × 50g ball of Rowan Summer Tweed, rush (A)
1 × mixed hank of Stef Francis embroidery thread, colour 07 (B)
4.00mm (F/5) crochet hook
Handle from www.u-handbag.com

Size

Width 19cm (7¹/₂in); depth 15cm (6in)

Tension

15 sts × 12 rows to 10cm (4in) over patt using 4.00mm (G/6) hook.

Abbreviations

dc double crochet
ss slip stitch
st(s) stitch(es)
tr treble
yrh yarn around hook

Special abbreviations

dc2tog – insert hook into next st, yrh, draw a loop through; rep into the next st, yrh, draw through all loops on hook.
MB – make bobble, leaving last loop of each tr on hook work 5tr into back loop of next st, yrh and draw through all 6 loops.

FRONT

Using 1 strand of each yarn together, make 30ch.

Row 1: 1dc into 2nd ch from hook, 1dc into each ch to end, turn. (29 dc)

Row 2: 3ch, miss first dc, working into back loops work 1tr into next dc, [MB in next dc, 1tr into each of next 2dc] to end, turn.

Row 3: 1ch, working into front loops work 1dc into first tr, 1dc into each st to end, turn.

Row 4: As Row 2.

Row 5: As Row 3 working dc2tog 3 times evenly accross. (3 sts decreased)

Row 6: As Row 2.

Rows 7 and 8: As Rows 3 and 4.

Rows 9–16: Work Rows 5 and 6 four times, varying positions of dc2tog on each dec row.

Work 6 rows dc.

Fasten off.

BACK

Using A only, work as front.

BOBBLE

Using A only, make 4ch, 12tr into 4th ch from hook, ss into top of 3ch.

Next row: 2ch, [leaving last loop of each tr on hook work 1tr into each of next 4tr, yrh and draw through all 5 loops] 3 times, 6ch.

Fasten off.

Stuff bobble with scraps of yarn, then join in opening.

MAKING UP

Leaving top 6cm (2¹/₄in) open at each side, join sides and lower edge. Fold top 3 rows of back and front over a handle and sew down. Join ch of bobble to top of one side.

The textures and colours in this bag remind me of lazy summer days in the sun

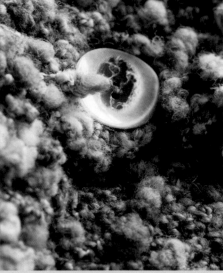

Materials
4 x 50g balls of Adriafil Graphic
3.50mm (E/4) crochet hook
Large button
Magnetic bag catch

Size
Width: 31cm (12¹/₂in); depth 18cm (7in).

Tension
14 dc x 17 rows to 10cm (4in) using
3.50mm (E/4) hook.

Abbreviations
alt alternate
ch chain
cont continue
dc double crochet
dec decrease
inc increase
rep repeat
RS right side
ss slip stitch
st(s) stitch(es)
tch turning chain
tr treble
WS wrong side

Special abbreviations
dc2tog – double crochet 2 sts together,
insert hook into next st, wrap yarn around
hook, draw a loop through; rep this step
into the next st (3 loops on the hook),
yarn around hook and draw through all
3 loops on the hook to complete.
tr2tog – treble crochet 3 sts together,
wrap yarn around hook, insert hook into
next st, wrap yarn around hook, draw a
loop through, wrap yarn and draw through
2 of loops on hook (2 loops left on hook);
rep this step into next st (3 loops on
hook), wrap yarn and draw through all
3 loops on hook to complete.

retro clutch bag

This glorious yarn just called out to me, asking to be made
into something unusual and desirable. Here is a great little
clutch bag with retro styling, which makes the best of its
textures and colours. It's made in one piece, so there is
minimal sewing to do at the end.

BAG
(Worked in one piece)
Front
Make 37ch.
Row 1: 1dc into 2nd ch from hook,
1dc into each ch to end, turn. (36 dc)
Row 2: 1ch, 1dc into each st to end,
turn.
Rep last row once more.
Row 3 (inc row): 1ch, 1dc into first
st, 2dc into next st, 1dc into each st
to last 2 sts, 2dc into next st, 1dc into
last st, turn.
Work 5 rows dc.
Rep last 6 rows 3 times. (44 dc)
Mark each end of last row.
Cont straight until work measures
18cm (7in).
Mark each end of last row.
Gussets
Leave main piece of work, cut a
length of yarn and attach tp tch of
last row, make 28ch.
Fasten off.
Cont with main yarn.
Next row: Make 29ch, 1dc into 2nd
ch from hook, 1dc into each ch, 1dc
into each dc of main bag, 1dc into
each ch to end, turn. (100 dc)
Work in dc until gusset measures
5cm (2in).
Fasten off.
Next row: Miss first 28dc, rejoin
yarn to next dc, 1ch, 1dc into this st
and foll 43 sts, turn. (44 dc)

Work straight in dc for the same
number of rows (or the same
measurement) as between markers
on front.
Work a further 3 rows as set.
Next row (dec row): 1ch, 1dc in first
dc, dc2tog over next 2 sts, 1dc into
each st to last 3 sts, dc2tog over next
2 sts, 1dc into last st, turn.
Work 5 rows of dc.
Rep last 6 rows 3 times. (36 sts)
Cont straight until work measures
41cm (16in), dec 4 sts evenly across
last row. (32 sts)
Front flap
Every row is worked with RS facing
– do not turn at end of rows.
Row 1: 3ch (count as 1tr), miss first
st, 1tr into each st to end. (32 sts)
Row 2: Work from left to right
working into front loop of each st,
*7ch, ss into next tr; rep from *
ending 7ch, ss into top of 3ch.
Row 3 (inc row): 3ch, (count as 1tr),
miss first tr, working into back loops
of last tr row work 2tr into next st,
*1tr into each st to last 2 sts, 2tr into
next st, 1tr into last st. (34 tr)
Row 4: As Row 2.
Rep last 2 rows once more. (36 sts)
Row 7: 3ch (count as 1tr), miss first
st, working into back loops of last tr
row work 1tr into each st.
Row 8: As Row 2.
Rep last 2 rows once more.

Tips

● The button on the front of this bag is just for show – it closes with a magnetic fastening that is attached behind. Choose a very decorative button in quite a large size for best effect.

● This yarn has the most wonderful texture and comes in a range of exciting colours. It is not that easy to work with at first but persevere – the results are more than worth the effort.

● You can line this bag if you wish – use the finished crochet piece as a 'pattern' to cut the fabric, but remember to allow extra all round for the seams. The magnetic catch can either be stitched in place on the lining, or you can stitch it in place first so the lining covers it; the magnet should be strong enough to work through a thin layer of fabric.

Flap shaping
Row 1: 3ch (count as 1tr), miss first st, working into back loops of last tr row work tr2tog over next 2 sts, 1tr into next 12 sts, tr2tog over next 2 sts, 1tr into next st. (16 sts) Work on these sts only.
Row 2: As Row 2 of main flap pattern.
Dec in this way on next and foll 2 alt rows.

Work 2nd row again.
Fasten off.**
With RS facing, rejoin yarn to first st after first side and work from ** to **.

MAKING UP

With RS together, sew gussets in place. Turn to RS. Sew button to centre of flap shaping.
Attach the magnetic fastening behind the button, by stitching each half to a circle of stiff fabric first, then stitch this to the inside of the bag to correspond with the button position.

going to tea bag

Scenes from nature and architecture often inspire me and the 'going to tea' bag shape came from a circular staircase in a hotel where I stayed once, in the county of Yorkshire in northern England.

Materials

1 × 50g ball of Debbie Bliss Maya, soft green (A)
1 × 50g ball of Colinette Enigma, green (B)
1 × rose handle from u-handbags.com
4.00mm (F/5) crochet hook

Size

Width 23cm (9in); depth 18cm (7in).

Tension

Tension is not important for this project.

Abbreviations

ch chain
dc double crochet
dtr double treble
htr half treble
ss slip stitch
tr treble

BACK

Using A, make 4ch, ss into first ch to form a ring.

Work 8dc into ring.

Cont in a spiral, working into back loop of each st. 1htr into each of 5dc, 2tr into each of next 13 sts, 2dtr into each of next 7 sts, *1dtr into next st, 2dtr into next st; rep from * until bag measures 18cm (7in) across.

Fasten off.

FRONT

Work as back using 1 strand A and B together.

FRILL

With back facing, join back and front together, working into both loops of back and back loop of front. 4ch, *2dtr into next st, 1dtr into next st; rep from * around just over half of outer edge.

Fasten off.

MAKING UP

Backstitch through both thicknesses at base of frill. Turn over top edge to form a straight line. Attach handles as per manufacturer's instructions.

Tips

● Using two strands of yarn together is great to add more texture and bulk to your projects. Always make sure the yarns blend or contrast in colour and have differing textures for more effect.

● Sewing the bag together with slip stitch is a quick and easy way of making it up and is the best method for this design and the edge wanted.

● When choosing a handle check the size of the opening carefully before sewing up. The handle used for this bag, like many, needs no glueing or sewing – it uses clasps to hold the crochet.

● Always keep interesting handles from old bags to reuse in your new designs.

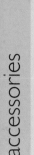

zig zag bag

The architecture of Barcelona, with its well-defined shapes and colours, gave me the first ideas for this bag. Colours from comic books provided the rest of my inspiration. Great fun to make and use!

Materials

1 x 100g ball of South West Trading Optimum DK, colour 560 bubble gum (A)
1 x 100g ball of Bouton d'Or Flash, serpolet (B)
1 x 100g ball of Ironstone Glisseen, colour ng/7 (C)
3.50mm (E/4) crochet hook
Decorative rose button
Magnetic catch

Size

Width: 18cm (7in); depth 14cm (5½in).

Gauge

1 patt rep of 16 sts measures 9cm (3½in) wide using 3.50mm (E/4) crochet hook.

Abbreviations

ch chain
ch sp chain space
cont continue
dc double crochet
dtr double treble
patt pattern
rep repeat
st(s) stitch(es)
tr treble
yrh yarn round hook

Special abbreviations

tr3tog – wrap yarn around hook, insert hook into next st, wrap yarn around hook, draw a loop through, wrap yarn and draw through 2 loops on hook (2 loops left on hook); rep this step into next st (3 loops on hook), rep this step into next st (4 loops on hook), wrap yarn and draw through all four loops on hook to complete.

BACK AND FRONT ALIKE

Using A, make 36ch.
Row 1: Using A, 1tr into 4th ch from hook, *1tr into each of next 6ch, tr3tog over next 3ch, 1tr into each of next 6ch, *[1tr, 1ch, 1tr] into next ch; rep from * to * once, 2tr into last ch, turn.
Row 2: Using B, 3ch, work into front loop of each st, 1tr into first tr, *1tr into each of next 6tr, tr3tog over next 3sts, 1tr into each of next 6tr, *[1tr, 1ch, 1tr] in 1ch sp; rep from * to * once more, 2tr in 3rd of 3ch, turn.
Row 3: Using C, 3ch, work into back loop of each st, 1tr into first tr, *1tr into each of next 6tr, tr3tog over next 3sts, 1tr into each of next 6tr, *[1tr, 1ch, 1tr] in 1ch sp; rep from * to * once, 2tr in 3rd of 3ch, turn.
Rows 2 and 3 form patt.

Cont in patt in stripes of 2 rows A, [1 row C, 1 row A] twice, 2 rows C and 1 row B.
Fasten off.
Join sides and base.

HANDLE

Using A and C tog, make 4ch, ss in first ch to form a ring.
5dc into ring.
Work in continuous rounds of ss, working into front loop only of each st, until handle measures 22cm (8½in).
Fasten off.

EDGING

Using C.
First petal: *4ch, miss 3ch, [3tr, 3ch, 1ss] in next ch;
2nd petal: 5ch, miss 3ch, [1tr, 3dtr, 1tr, 3ch, 1ss] in next ch;

The well-defined shapes and the colours of the architecture of Barcelona has inspired this fun bag

3rd petal: 5ch, miss 3ch, [3tr, 3ch, 1ss] in next ch; 6ch; rep from *until edging fits along base, omitting 6ch at end of last rep.
Fasten off.
Make another strip to match.

MAKING UP

Sew edging strips to base of bag. Sew handle in place. Sew button to centre top of front and use ch sp of centre top of back as buttonhole.

Tips

● If you do not want to use a crochet cord for this bag there are many different types of handle available from specialist websites such as u-handbags.com or bagsofhandles.co.uk.

● The rose button used in this project is a special one chosen for this bag. Look out for interesting buttons in specialist stores and on internet sites.

● The button is decorative – the bag is secured with a magnetic catch stitched inside. If you want to use the button but do not want to make a buttonhole in the flap, make a short crochet chain to slip over the button instead.

Materials
4 × 50g balls of Lana Grossa Pashmina,
colour 14 grey (A)
1 × 50g ball of Lana Grossa Pashmina,
colour 05 pink (B)
4.00mm (F/5) crochet hook
3.50mm (E/4) crochet hook

Size
To fit an average hot water bottle:
width: 29cm (11½in); length 38cm (15in),
including top gathering.

Tension
20dc × 26 rows to 10cm (4in) over double
crochet, using 4.00mm (F/5) hook.

Abbreviations
ch chain
ch sp chain space
dc double crochet
RS right side
ss slip stitch
st(s) stitch(es)
tog together
tr treble
WS wrong side

hot water bottle cover

There's nothing so warm and cosy on a cold winter's night as being able to snuggle up to a toasty hot water bottle. And here is the perfect cover to make your bottle look smart and sophisticated enough for any inspection!

FRONT AND BACK

(both alike)
Using 4.00mm (F/5) hook and MC, make 59ch.
Row 1 (RS): 1dc into 2nd ch from hook, 1dc into each ch to end, turn. (58 dc)
Next row: 1ch, 1dc into each dc to end, turn.
Rep last row until work measures 5cm (2in), ending with a WS row.
****Change to B, do not cut A but carry it up side of work.
Work two rows dc in B.
Cut off B.****
Cont in A until work measures 22cm (8¾in), ending with a WS row.
Work from ** to **.
Cont in A until work measures 28cm (11in), ending with a WS row.
Eyelet row: 3ch (count as 1tr), miss first dc, 1tr into next dc, [1ch, miss next dc, 1tr into each of next 3dc] to end.
Next row: 1ch, 1dc into each tr and each ch sp, ending with 1dc into top of 3ch, turn.
Cont in dc until work measures 38cm (15in).
Fasten off.

MAKING UP

With RS tog and using 3.50mm (E/4) hook, join A to top of side edge. Join sides and lower edge by working 1 row of dc through both thicknesses. Turn to RS.
Top edging
Using 3.50mm (E/4) hook and A, starting at top side seam and working all around top edge, work the foll:
1ch, [1dc, 3ch, 1dc] into first dc, *miss next dc, [1dc, 3ch, 1dc] into next dc; rep from * ending with miss next dc, ss into first dc.
Fasten off.

CORD

Using 4.00mm (F/5) hook and A double, make a 100cm (40in) length of ch. Working into 2nd ch from hook and each ch to end, ss back along the length of ch placing the hook into the strand on the reverse side of each ch. Fasten off and sew in ends.

Beginning at centre front, thread the
cord through the eyelets. Pull the ties
together and tie in a neat bow to
form a snug fit around the neck of
the bottle.

lavender bag

The smell of lavender is always evocative of warm summer days and there is nothing nicer than sliding between crisp cotton sheets surrounded by the delicate scent of these flowers. This little bag is decorated with a stitched ribbon flower for that perfect finishing touch.

Materials
1 × 25g ball of Twilleys Crochet cotton, cream (A)
1 × 25g ball of Anny Blatt Victoria ribbon (B)
3.50mm (E/4) crochet hook

Size
Depth 13cm (5in); width at lower edge 11cm (4¼in).

Tension
25 dc to 10cm (4in) using 3.50mm (E/4) crochet hook.

Abbreviations
ch chain
dc single crochet
inc increase
rep repeat
RS right side
ss slip stitch
st(s) stitch(es)
tr treble
WS wrong side

BACK
Beg at top edge. Using 3.50mm (E/4) hook and A, make 24ch.
Row 1 (RS): 1dc into 2nd ch from hook, 1dc to end, turn. (23 dc)
Work into back loop of st throughout.
Row 2: 1ch, 1dc into each st to end, turn.
Rep Row 2 twice.
Eyelet row: 1ch, 1dc into first dc, [1ch, miss 1dc, 1dc into next dc] to end, turn*
Rep Row 2 until work measures 9cm (3½in) from beg, end with WS row.
Work 2 rows dc in B.
Next row: Carry colour not in use loosely across WS.
1ch, work in dc working 4A, 5B, 5A, 5B and 4A.
**Next row (inc): With B, 1ch, 1tr into each of first 2dc, [2dc into next dc, 1dc into each of next 5dc]

3 times, 2dc into next dc, 1dc into each of last 2dc, turn. (27 dc)
Work 1 row dc with A and 2 rows B. Fasten off.

FRONT
Work as back to *.
Rep row 2 until front measures same as back to inc row. Complete as back from **.

DRAWSTRING
Using B, make a 60cm (24in) length of ch. Fasten off.

MAKING UP
Using B, make chain stitch flowers on front. Join A to top left corner, 5ch, ss into corner, 7ch, ss into same place, 5ch, ss into same place. Fasten off. Join sides and lower edge from eyelet row. Thread drawstring and tie.

travel slippers

Once again the colour for these pretty pumps was inspired by the plants and flowers in my own garden. The colours of the fading delphiniums in the border just sparked the idea – the clear blues of early summer change and turn a bluey lilac as the season progresses.

Materials
2 x 50g balls of Lang Soft Shetland, colour 1057 (A)
Small amount of Trendsetter Merino Sie, lilac
Small amount of Trendsetter Merino Sie, olive
3.50mm (E/4) crochet hook
Pair of polystyrene shoe lasts

Size
To fit UK shoe size 4–5.

Tension
Tension is not important for this project, as the slippers are felted to fit.

Abbreviations
ch chain
ch sp chain space
dc double crochet
htr half treble
ss slip stitch
st(s) stitch(es)
tr treble
yrh yarn around hook

Special abbreviations
tr2tog – wrap yarn around hook, insert hook into next st, wrap yarn around hook, draw a loop through, wrap yarn and draw through 2 loops on hook (2 loops left on hook); rep this step into next st (3 loops on hook), wrap yarn and draw through all loops on hook to complete.

SOLES
(Make 2 and flip for right and left foot)
Using A, make 16ch.
Row 1: 1tr into 4th ch from hook, 1tr into each ch to end, turn. (14 sts)
Row 2: 3ch, 1tr into first tr, 1tr into each tr, 2tr into top of 3ch, turn. (16 sts)
Rows 3–4: 3ch, miss first tr, 1tr int each tr, 1tr into top of 3ch, turn.
Rows 5–6: 3ch, miss first tr, tr2tog, 1tr into each tr to last 3 sts, tr2tog, 1tr into top of 3ch, turn. (12 sts)
Rows 7–9: 3ch, 2tr in first tr, 2tr in next tr, 1tr in each tr, 1tr in top of 3ch, turn.
Row 10: 3ch, 1tr in first tr, 1tr in each tr, 1tr in top of 3ch, turn. (22 sts)
Row 11: As Row 7. (25 sts)
Row 12: As Row 10. (26 sts)
Rows 13–16: 3ch, miss first tr, 1tr in each tr, 1tr into top of 3ch, turn.
Row 18: 3ch, mist first tr, tr2tog, [1tr in next tr, 2trtog] 7 times, tr2tog. (17 sts)
Fasten off.

TOPS
(Make 2)
Work from top down towards soles.
Using A, make 71ch, ss in first ch to form a ring.
Round 1: 1dc in next 20ch, 1htr in next 10ch, 1tr in next 5ch, [2tr, 1ch, 2tr] in next ch (this is the toe), 1tr in next 5ch, 1htr in next 10ch, 1dc in next 20ch, ss in first dc, turn. (75 sts)
Round 2: 1ch, 1dc in next 20dc, 1htr in next 10htr, 1tr in next 7tr [2tr, 1ch, 2tr] in 1ch sp, 1tr in next 7tr, 1htr in next 10htr, 1dc in next 20 dc, ss in first dc, turn. (79 sts)
Round 3: 1ch, 1dc in next 20dc, 1htr in next 10htr, 1tr in next 9htr, [2tr, 1ch, 2tr] in 1ch sp, 1tr in next 9tr, 1htr in next 10htr, 1dc in next 20 dc, ss in first dc, turn. (83 sts)
Round 4: 1ch, 1dc in next 20dc, 1htr in next 10htr, 1tr in next 11tr, [2tr, 1ch, 2tr] in 1ch sp, 1tr in next 11tr, 1htr in next 10htr, 1dc in next 20dc, ss in first dc, turn. (87 sts)
Back of heel
1dc in next 19dc, ss in next st, turn, 1dc in next 38sts, ss in next st, turn, 1dc in next 19sts.
Fasten off.

Notes
Yarn is used double throughout – pull one end from inside of one ball and one from outside and hold together.

The slippers will look enormous as you finish them but this is correct – they shrink down in size when felted so do not worry.

TWISTS

(Make 4 in A and 1 each in scraps of other colours, varying length of ch each time)

Make approx 25ch.

Row 1: Miss 1ch, 2dc in each ch. Fasten off.

MAKING UP

Attach tops to soles by overstitching along edges.

FELTING

Place the ballet slippers on the last then put a pop sock over each one and tie to hold everything in place. Place the slippers in the washing machine on a hot wash.

Try pumps on after one wash – if still too big or not shrunk to shoe last, give one more wash on the last.

Leave the pumps on the last until completely dry.

Stitch twists to top of slipper.

Tips

● For successful machine felting you will need to know your machine well. Knit a few swatches, measure them, then try felting at different settings to see how much they shrink. These slippers should shrink by 25–30%.

● The slippers can also be felted by hand. Fill a large bowl with hot water and soap and wear rubber gloves to protect your hands. Immerse the item fully. Rub gently all over the surface with your hands, gently squeezing the water out every so often, then begin the process again. Repeat until the item is the size you would like it to be, using the polystyrene lasts for the last stages to get the correct shape. Be careful with any subsequent washes, or the item may felt more and thus shrink further.

● Use liquid soap when felting, not detergent. Soap helps the water soak into the fibres so they open up and felt better.

● Place an old lint-free towel in the machine along with the slippers to help create more friction. Items also felt better in the machine if they are not enclosed in a bag.

The bluey-lilac of late summer delphiniums inspired these pretty and oh-so-soft travel slippers

his & hers cushion

This cushion is so easy to make but it's full of texture and vibrant colour. The pattern is for a square cushion but you can make the same design into a rectangular shape if you like by working more multiples of the rows.

Materials
10 x 50g balls of Gedifra Colorito, colour 6946
5.00mm (H/8) crochet hook
30cm (12in) square cushion pad

Size
30cm (12in) square.

Tension
13 sts x 20 rows to 10cm (4in) over patt using 5.00mm (H/8) hook.

Abbreviations
ch chain
dc double crochet
patt pattern
rep repeat
RS right side
st(s) stitch(es)
WS wrong side

Notes
Yarn is used double throughout, changing combinations at random, carrying yarns not in use loosely up side of work.

CUSHION FRONT AND BACK
(Both alike).
Make 41ch.
Row 1 (WS): 1dc into 2nd ch from hook, 1dc into each ch to end, turn. (40 dc)
Row 2: 1ch, 1dc into dc, turn.
Row 3: As Row 2.
Row 4: 1ch, *[1dc into dc 3 rows below next dc] 5 times, 1dc into each of next 5dc; rep from * to end, turn.

Row 5: As Row 2.
Row 6: 1ch, *1dc into each of next 5dc, [1dc into dc 3 rows below next dc] 5 times to end, turn.
Rep Rows 3 to 6 until work measures 30cm (12in).
Fasten off.

MAKING UP
With RS tog, join 3 sides, turn to RS, insert cushion pad then join remaining side.

Tips

● Cushion pads come in a wide variety of shapes and sizes. The pattern is designed for one 30cm (12in) square, so if your cushion is bigger you will need to adjust the pattern to suit. As long as you keep making multiples of the basic pattern of 47 double crochet and 6 rows this should not be a problem. Remember that a bigger cushion will need more yarn!

● Use quite a firm cushion pad for these cushions to make the most of the wonderful texture across the surface.

materials and techniques

Crochet is very versatile and all you need are a few basic materials and to know how to work the few simple stitches that in different combinations can be used to work any crochet pattern. This section gives details of everything you will need and also explains the basic techniques.

yarns & hooks

Although there are special crochet yarns available, you can crochet with any yarn suitable for knitting as well – and even with fine wire. There are beautiful materials available now – see the back of this book for suppliers.

Crochet hooks vary in size and are most often available in plastic or aluminium. Some pattern books give hook sizes in different formats, so the handy conversion chart (right) will help you find the right size.

Crochet hook conversions

Metric (mm)	US size	UK/Canada (old) Wool	Cotton
0.60	No. 14 steel	-	7
0.75	No. 12 steel	-	6½
1.00	No. 10 steel	-	5½
1.25	No. 9 steel	-	4½
1.50	No. 8 steel	16	3½
1.75	No. 7 steel	15	2½
2.00	B/1	14	1½
2.50	C/2	12	0
3.00	D/3	11	3
3.50	E/4	9	4
4.00	F/5	8	5
4.50	G/6	7	
5.00	H/8	6	
5.50	I/9	5	
6.00	J/10	4	
6.50	K10 ½	3	
7.00	K10 ½	2	
8.00	L/12	0	
9.00	M/13	00	
10.00	N/15	000	
12.00	N/15	000	
15.00	N/15	000	
17.00	N/15	000	
25.00	N/15	000	
35.00	N/15	000	

Yarn conversions

25g	⅞oz
50g	1¾oz
100g	3½oz

Yarns are listed with their NM number to describe their yardage. This number states how many metres of yarn will come from 1 gram weight, so for example a single ply 1/28 yarn will give 28 metres per gram whilst 2/28 will give half that (because it is twice as thick). The table below gives the yardage, needle sizes and stitches per inch.

Weight	(Tex)	Yards per 150g cone (approx)	Needle size, stocking stitch	Needle size, lace	US crochet hook size	Stitches per inch (guide)
lace	1/14 or 2/28 (or 70 Tex)	2,300	Many people use several strands of this together for hand knitting	US 2–5, 2.50–3.75mm, old UK 12–9	8 or 9	7–8
4 ply	2/14 (or 140 Tex)	1,150	US 0–1, 2.00–2.75mm, old UK 14–12	US 5–7, 3.75–4.50mm, old UK 9–7	B/1	
fingering	3/14 (or 50/140 Tex)	770	US 3–5, 3.00–3.75mm, old UK 11–9	US 8–9, 5.50–6.00mm, old UK 6–4	C/2	6–7
doubleknit (dk)	4/14 (or 140/140 Tex)	570	US 5–6, 3.75–4.00mm, old UK 9–8		D/3	5–6
aran	8/14	285	US 7–8, 4.50–5.00mm, old UK 7–6			
chunky	12/14	190	US 8–10, 5.00–6.00mm, old UK 6–4			

Roughly, 300–350g of the lace weight or 4 ply should make a pullover – thicker yarns will need extra weight for the same garment so, for example, a DK weight pullover might need 500g. Amounts below 200g are better for scarves, gloves, baby clothes etc.

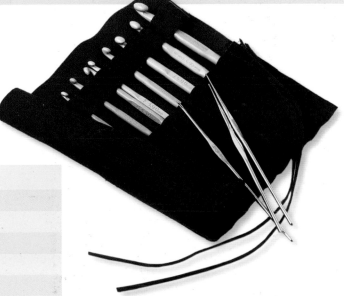

18+ wpi is Lace = 2600+ yards per pound

16 wpi is Fingering = 1900 to 2400 yards per pound

14 wpi is Sport = 1200 to 1800 yards per pound

12 wpi is Worsted = 900 to 1200 yards per pound

10 wpi is Bulky = 600 to 800 yards per pound

8 or less wpi is Very Bulky = 400 to 500 yards per pound

basic stitches

In crochet the left hand tensions the yarn and holds the work while the right hand uses the hook. The following show the basic techniques, but use your own methods if you are familiar with them.

Abbreviations

alt	alternate
beg	beginning
bet	between
bl	back of loop
CC	contrasting colour
ch	chain
ch sp	chain space
cm	centimetre
cont	continues
dc	double crochet
dec	decrease
fl	front of loop
foll	following/follows
g	gram
hdc	half double crochet
htr	half treble
inc	increase
MC	main colour
m	marker
mm	millimetre
patt	pattern
pm	place marker
rem	remaining
rep	repeat
RS	right side
sc	single crochet
sl st	slip stitch
st(s)	stitch(es)
tch	turning chain
tr	treble
WS	wrong side
yrh	yarn round hook

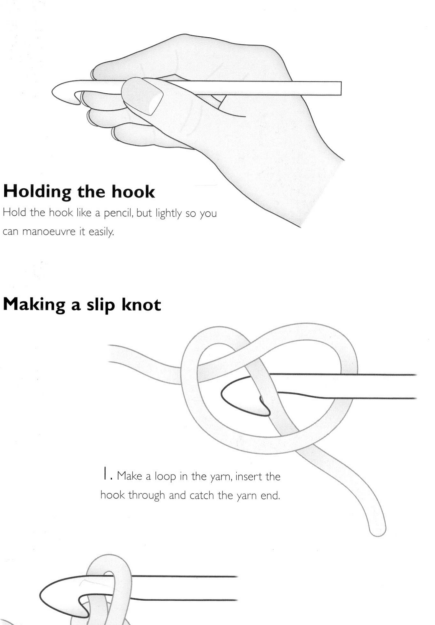

Holding the hook

Hold the hook like a pencil, but lightly so you can manoeuvre it easily.

Making a slip knot

1. Make a loop in the yarn, insert the hook through and catch the yarn end.

2. Pull the yarn through to make a loop, then gently pull on both ends to tighten the loop on the hook.

Chain stitch

1. With the hook in front of the yarn, take the yarn round the hook from the back to the front and catch the yarn. This basic movement is called yarn round hook.

2. Bring the yarn through the loop on the hook to make a new chain loop on the hook.

Slip stitch

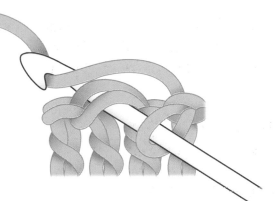

Insert the hook into the stitch and take the yarn round the hook. Draw a new loop through both the stitch and the loop on the hook, ending with one loop on the hook.

Double crochet

1. Insert the hook into the second chain from hook, yarn round hook and pull a loop through.

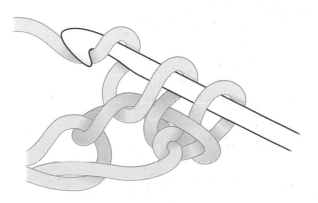

2. Wrap the yarn round the hook and pull a loop through both loops. One loop remains on the hook – 1 dc made.

Half treble

1. Wrap the yarn around the hook and insert into third chain from hook.

2. Pull a loop through this chain – you now have three loops on the hook. Wrap the yarn around the hook again. Pull through all three loops on the hook.

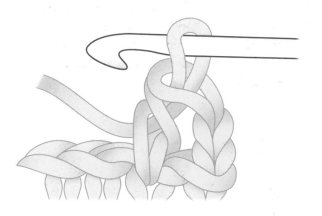

3. One loop remains on the hook – 1 htr made.

treble crochet

1. Wrap the yarn around the hook and insert into fourth chain from hook. Pull a loop through this chain, you now have three loops on the hook, wrap the yarn around the hook again. Pull through all three loops on the hook.

2. Draw through the first two loops only and wrap the yarn again.

3. Draw through the last two loops on the hook. One loop remains on the hook – 1 tr made.

Working longer stitches

Double treble, triple treble, and so on are all worked in the same way as a treble, but with one more wrapping of the yarn round the hook for each longer stitch, giving one more step when drawing through two loops at a time.

Here's the number of times to wrap the yarn round the hook when making these longer stitches.

Type of Stitch	Number of times to wrap
Double treble	two
Triple treble	three
Quadruple treble	four
Quintuple treble	five

Fastening off

After the last stitch pull another loop through, cut the yarn, and pull the end through.

beads

Beads are seductive! Walking into any bead supply store is like entering another world and one visit to an internet search engine will reveal many sources. Do not forget, however, that if you purchase beads from overseas, you may be charged import duty and tax. It is always good to contact these firms before you buy and ask if they already have a supplier in your own country.

wire

Wire is available in many different thicknesses and gauges, ranging from gauge 8 (the thickest) to gauge 34 (the thinnest). It also comes in different metals and coatings. Enamelled copper wire is less expensive than silver-plated wire. The colour of the base wire affects the finished colour: pink enamel applied to silver wire looks brighter than the same pink enamel applied to copper, for example.

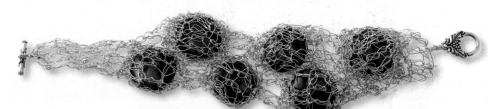

findings

Findings is a general term used to describe ready-made components such as chains, clasps, brooch bars, and earwires. They are readily available from jewellery suppliers, and craft and hobby stores. Findings come in many different finishes – shiny and matt, antique-effect metallic, and so on. Always choose one that both complements the colour of the wire and beads that you are using and the style of the piece. Magnetic clasps make a quick-and-easy fastening for a bracelet – but I never use them on necklaces for safety reasons, as other metallic objects can sometimes be attracted to the magnet.

index

suppliers

Most suppliers required for the projects included in this book may be found at your local craft or yarn shop. For speciality products, check the websites listed here.

YARN COMPANIES

Adriafil Yarns
www.adriafil.com for stockists

Anny Blatt
www.annyblatt.com for stockists

Debbie Bliss
www.debbieblissonline.com

Bouton D'or
www.boutondor.com

Coats Craft Rowan Yarns
www.coatscrafts.co.uk

Colinette Yarns
www.colinette.com for stockists

Gedifra
Available from
www.paviyarns.co.uk

Knitglobal
www.knitglobal.com

Lana Grossa
www.lanagrossa.com
for stockists

Lanartus Yarns
www.lanartus.net

Lang Yarns
www.langyarns.ch/en
for stockists

Louisa Harding
www.louisaharding.co.uk

Noro Yarns
www.noroyarns.com
for stockists

Patons Yarns
www.patonsyarns.co.uk

Presencia
Available from
www.paviyarns.co.uk

RY Classic Yarns
www.ryclassic.com

Sirdar Yarns
www.sirdar.co.uk

South West Trading Company
(SWTC) Yarns
www.soysilk.com

Stef Francis
www.stef-francis.co.uk

Trendsetter Yarns
www.trendsetteryarns.com

Twilleys of Stamford
www.twilleys.co.uk for stockists

Wensleydale Longwool
www.wensleydalelongwoolsheep
shop.co.uk

STOCKISTS

Designer Yarns
www.designeryarns.co.uk

Get Knitted
www.getknitted.co.uk

Pavi Yarns
www.paviyarns.co.uk
Stockists of Knitglobal,
Trendsetter, Presencia, Gedifra
and Lanartus yarns

Wingham Wool Work
www.winghamwoolwork.co.uk

WIRE

Scientific Wires
www.wires.co.uk

BAG TRIMMINGS
AND HANDLES

Bags of Handles
www.bagsofhandles.co.uk

U Handbags
www.u-handbag.com

BEADS AND BUTTONS

Beads Direct
www.beadsdirect.co.uk

The Button Company
www.buttoncompany.co.uk

Injabulo
www.injabulo.com

acknowledgements

Another journey, this time with one pin – the crochet hook.

I have enjoyed searching for less well used stitches to incorporate into the designs in this book, and have learnt a lot en route as well. As always my inspirations for design and colours start in my sketch book.

My special thanks must go to Cindy Richards who has faith in my abilities and helps turn dreams into books. Thanks also to all CICO staff in London and to the photographer Paul Bricknall who made the shoot enjoyable and produced good images.

Marie Clayton, my editor, with whom I had a cyber relationship, thank you.
Stylist Sue Rowlands; thank you, the book looks great.
Designer Roger Hammond; thank you. I love the look you have created.

Thank you to all the yarn companies who supported me and special thanks go to Karen and Paul at Pavi yarns who always knew where to find just what I needed; thank you both.

Sian Brown; thank you for your dedication to this book and its timeline and help with patterns, which leads me on to a special thank you to Jenny Shore who I think can read my mind, or at least reads my designs well. Thank you Jenny and thanks for the beautiful craftsmanship you portrayed in the items for the book.

Also to Shiela Grudzinski, owner of my local yarn shop, who again is always there to help, and produced a beautiful piece of work for this book, thank you Shiela.

It has not been a easy year but as always my family are my rock, so to:
My husband Nigel, who still has patience in having a creative wife and is still calm, loving and shares my dreams; thank you darling, I could not do it without you.

James and Emma, my duo in whom I have unmeasurable pride, inspire me, believe in me and do make life so much fun, thank you both.

Not least Linda, my treasure, who also has utter patience with me and the yarn, beads, looms, wheels, needles and pins that I seem to surround myself with, and who keeps my home an oasis of utter calm, thank you.

MJH – as always my tomorrows are your gift, thank you.

To all of you who wishing you could, or had, or did – do it.

Take hold of your dream
Catch onto that star
Have faith in yourself
You are what you are.

Chrissie Day